Confession

Confession

Doorway to Forgiveness

Jim Forest

ORBIS BOOKS
Maryknoll, New York 10545

Founded in 1970, Orbis Books endeavors to publish works that enlighten the mind, nourish the spirit, and challenge the conscience. The publishing arm of the Maryknoll Fathers & Brothers, Orbis seeks to explore the global dimensions of the Christian faith and mission, to invite dialogue with diverse cultures and religious traditions, and to serve the cause of reconciliation and peace. The books published reflect the views of their authors and do not represent the official position of the Maryknoll Society. To learn more about Maryknoll and Orbis Books, please visit our website at www.maryknoll.com.

Library of Congress Cataloging-in-Publication Data

Forest, Jim.
    Confession : doorway to forgiveness / Jim Forest.
        p. cm.
    ISBN 1-57075-386-5 (pbk.)
    1. Confession. I. Title.

    BV845 .F67 2002
    264'.02086—dc21

                                                                    2001055462

To my grandchildren Zackary, Kara, and Noah,
direct descendants of Adam and Eve

And they were baptized by [John] in the river Jordan, confessing their sins.
—MATTHEW 3:6

But if you do not forgive, neither will your Father who is in heaven
forgive your trespasses.
—MARK 11:26

I will give you the keys of the kingdom of heaven,
and whatever you bind on earth shall be bound in heaven,
and whatever you loose on earth shall be loosed in heaven.
—MATTHEW 16:19

Many of those who believed came forward
confessing and divulging their deeds and practices.
—ACTS 19:18

Repent, and be baptized . . . in the name of Jesus Christ
for the forgiveness of your sins;
and you shall receive the gift of the Holy Spirit.
—ACTS 2:38

If we say we have no sin, we deceive ourselves and the truth is not in us.
If we confess our sins, he is faithful and just, and will forgive our sins.
—1 JOHN 1:8-9

Confess your sins to one another.
—JAMES 5:16

For it is better that a man should acknowledge his transgressions
than that he should harden his heart.
—ST. CLEMENT OF ROME, LETTER TO THE CORINTHIANS

Since we cannot live in this world without sin, the first hope we have
of salvation is through confession, nor should anyone be so proud
as to claim that he is righteous in God's sight. The next step is love . . .
because love covers a multitude of sins.
— ST. BEDE THE VENERABLE, COMMENTARY ON THE FIRST LETTER OF JOHN

CONTENTS

INTRODUCTION

The tradition of confession, once common practice among Christians, fell on hard times but is today making a comeback. While confession is most easily found in the Orthodox Church, Catholics are increasingly finding their way back to this ancient practice. In Protestant churches various forms of spiritual guidance and counseling are on the rise, perhaps paving the way for the recovery of a lost sacrament. It seems likely that in another generation sacramental confession will not be so rare an event as it is today in the life of an ordinary Christian.

The purpose of this small book is to help revive confession where it has been abandoned or neglected, to help the reader prepare a better confession, and to help those who hear confessions better serve as Christ's witness, taking care not to impede the sacrament's healing strength. It is written by an Orthodox Christian who hopes it will be beneficial not only to Orthodox readers but also to Catholic and Protestant Christians.

Perhaps it is useful to say something about what led me to write a book on confession and what gives the book a broad Christian focus.

Growing up on the edge of a New Jersey town, Red Bank, my scattered childhood encounters with Christianity were chiefly with various forms of Protestantism in which sacramental confession didn't exist. Confession was among the "Romish" rituals long since rejected by those churches which had freed themselves from "the corruptions of Catholicism," a phrase that was not uncommon among Protestants in those days of religious cold war. In anti-

Catholic remarks I occasionally heard, confession was described
as a way Catholic priests deprived those who entered confessionals of their freedom. My Uncle Charles, who believed the Catholic
clergy longed to resume the torture and burning of heretics, was
convinced that confession was too easy: "It's the usual Catholic
hocus pocus. You just confess what you did and you're in the clear
to do it again and again and again." I heard from Protestants, "If
you have something to confess, confess it to God directly, and God
will forgive you. No priest is needed." (Yet later in life I came to
know Protestants, some of them pastors, who were deeply burdened with the memory of past sins, had yet to experience God's
forgiveness, and wished this dimension of sacramental life had not
been thrown away in the age of Reformation. Truly it was a case
of throwing out the baby with the bath water.)

When Protestant friends invited me to their churches, I went
quite willingly but was disinclined to memorize the Ten Commandments and found sermons infinitely boring. Sometimes I enjoyed the singing but too often churches seemed like classrooms
without blackboards. It was only when I was invited by a class-
mate to an Episcopal church at which there was a communion
service every Sunday that I found myself powerfully drawn to
Christianity. While I would walk a mile out of my way to avoid a
sermon, a sacrament-centered form of Christianity drew me with
the force of gravity. It was in this old church, where soldiers
wounded in the Revolutionary War had bled and died, that I was
baptized at the age of twelve. The priest, Fr. Levan, gave me a
special gift that day, an ancient Byzantine coin, on one side of
which was impressed the icon of Christ's haloed face—my first
encounter with the imagery of the Orthodox Church.

So far as I was aware, there was no practice of confession
within the parish, but in other respects it was a very traditional
form of Christianity I encountered at Christ Episcopal Church in
the village of Shrewsbury just south of Red Bank. Thanks to the
parish priest, I was made conscious of Christianity's origins in the
eastern Mediterranean. It was in this solidly American Protestant

community that I learned fragments of Greek, understanding that "Eucharist" meant "thanksgiving," "liturgy" meant "public work," and "Kyrie eleison" meant "Lord, have mercy."

That first period of church involvement lasted little more than a year. The main part of my teenage years was spent outside churches with no thought of sacraments or interest in the Bible. In my adolescent mind, Christianity became something for children and unadventurous adults. Nature was sacrament enough. Having moved to California, I took to the coastline and the mountains, biking and climbing during vacations, doing odd jobs, often sleeping under the stars. If there is a God, I thought, I will search for him by myself in the wilderness.

Later, out of high school and in the Navy, stationed in Washington, D.C., my religious search brought me back to Christianity. For half a year I was part of an Episcopal parish though visiting not only other Protestant churches but various Catholic churches as well. Having found myself most challenged both intellectually and spiritually by the Catholic Church, I started a course of instruction and in November 1960 became a Catholic, at the same time going to confession for the first time. Confession has ever since been an ordinary—but never easy—part of my life.

Two decades later, then living in Europe, my work took me to Moscow for a small theological conference hosted by the Russian Orthodox Church. In those days, the Soviet Union was showing no signs of giving up the ghost. The "iron curtain" was very solid and Communist symbols and slogans rarely out of sight once behind the curtain. While for twenty years I had occasionally read books and magazine articles about the Orthodox Church, the last thing I expected was that I was heading toward a life-changing encounter with Orthodox Christianity.

According to all I had read, the Orthodox Church in Russia was an ever-shrinking band of unlettered old women. True, old women were the majority in the church, but what old women! It was chiefly thanks to them that my vague interest in "Eastern" Christianity abruptly became far more intense. Attending the liturgy in one of Moscow's few open churches, I was overwhelmed by the climate of prayer generated by the worshipers—in my experience, only the black church in America came close. Seven years and many trips later, my wife and I were received into the Orthodox Church at a parish in Amsterdam, St. Nicholas of Myra.

I wasn't a "convert," I explained to bewildered Catholic friends at the time. I was only changing my address. The main event, my conversion to Christ, had started much earlier in my life. But nowhere else in Christianity had I experienced such depth and fervor of eucharistic life, such an intensity of prayer, such continuity of teaching, such a healthy capacity to resist passing ideological and theological fashions. For all of Orthodoxy's shortcomings—its "national churches," its jurisdictional rivalries, the inattention of so many Orthodox Christians to urgent social issues—I found it impossible not to be part of the Orthodox Church. Yet I felt and still feel a strong bond with the Catholic Church and a connection with anyone, no matter what his or her church, who is trying to follow Christ.

More than two-thirds of my life have now been spent in churches in which confession is recognized as a sacrament, even though in the Catholic Church it has been a sacrament in decline for the past quarter century, at least in North America and Western Europe.

In Holland, my home since 1977, I have yet to find a Catholic parish where confession is a visible part of church life. A few years ago I visited a large Catholic church near Utrecht erected in the fifties, a period of optimism about the community's future sacramental needs. Six confessionals had been built into its brick walls, but it had been years since a priest had sat in any of them. Each was being used as a closet—cleaning supplies in two of them, Mass booklets in another, candles in the next, assorted odds and ends in the last two, including a discarded Sacred Heart of Jesus statue.

One Dutch Catholic priest who avidly hoped for the sacrament's revival was the late Henri Nouwen, whom I had come to know when he was teaching at Yale. While in the Netherlands for a family visit in the early eighties, he took me one weekday morning to meet an elderly priest whom Henri admired both for his translations of the writings of Theresa of Avila and John of the Cross and because he was a good confessor. After being introduced in the church sacristy, I left the two of them alone so that Henri could make his confession. Half an hour later Henri reappeared, telling me with dismay that this was the first time in seven years that anyone had come to the pastor for such a purpose. "Can you imagine? Here is a man with a vocation not only to be a channel of God's forgiveness but also to give spiritual direction and wisdom. But no one wants it. It is like a town with a beautiful fountain that everyone ignores." I had rarely heard such grief in Henri's voice.

Yet even today there are Catholic churches with confessionals very much in use. Because my work often took me to London, in the years before becoming Orthodox I confessed regularly at that city's main Catholic church, Westminster Cathedral. Once, while in Rome for a meeting with Pope John Paul in 1980, I confessed at St. Peter's in one of the many confessionals in the back of that vast church. Last summer, while in England for an ecumenical conference, I visited a large and thriving parish in Birmingham, the Oratory, founded in the nineteenth century by Cardinal John Henry Newman. Here there were half-a-dozen confessionals standing ready for use. (Among those who attended Mass and went to confession at the Oratory in an earlier time was J.R.R. Tolkien when he was growing up. His *Lord of the Rings* trilogy has at its core one hobbit's struggle not to let temptation get the upper hand, a theme not unfamiliar to anyone going to confession.)

The vitality of confession in the Orthodox Church was not a decisive factor in my becoming Orthodox, yet I was always inspired when watching people confess in Orthodox parishes: priest and penitent standing before an icon of Christ, the person confessing toward the icon rather than the priest.

I was gradually to learn that the tradition of confession in the Orthodox Church was not only superficially different—standing rather than kneeling, in public view rather than hidden—but there is often a difference in emphasis. The geography of the ritual helped make it clear it was Christ who was being addressed by the person confessing and that the priest was chiefly a witness. There was a sense of familial intimacy in the closeness of penitent and priest standing so close to each other. Earlier in my life I had understood confession mainly as the listing of sins of which I was guilty. In the Orthodox Church I encountered a different emphasis: an attempt to identify what I had done that broke communion with God and my neighbor. It was a lesson I might have learned as a Catholic but I hadn't.

Little by little I came to better understand the great care one often notices in Orthodox parishes as believers prepare to receive communion—the awareness that communion with Christ requires being in a state of communion with those around us, and that it is a sin to go to the chalice if you are in a state of enmity.

Confession in One Parish

Orthodox parishes being relatively few in Holland and many of us living some distance away from our parish church, I am among those who go to confession before the liturgy on Sunday mornings rather than after Vespers Saturday night.

As is the Orthodox custom, confession usually occurs in a corner of the church not far from the altar. There is a narrow tilted stand on which are placed a New Testament and a cross. On the wall over the stand, illuminated by the flickering light of a *lampada* (an oil lamp), is an icon of Christ the Savior. Those wanting to confess stand in line, leaving enough space at the front so that the person confessing has a degree of privacy. While confession is going on, normally a reader recites psalms and prayers in the center of the church, thus preventing confessions from being audible.

Often the first person in line is Zacharia, a large, round-faced Ethiopian woman of a grandmotherly age with a faded cross tat-

tooed on her forehead. The priest receives her, as he does all penitents, by reciting words that remind her that he is only a witness
to the confession about to be made and that it is Christ the physician, invisibly present, who heals and forgives. Zacharia speaks
little Dutch, still less English, and not a word of Russian, Greek,
or German—thus no language that any of our priests understands.
It doesn't matter. She stands before the icon of Christ, her up-
raised hands rising and falling rhythmically, relating in her incomprehensible mother tongue whatever is burdening her. As the
priest grasps not a word of what she is saying, he does nothing
more than quietly recite the Jesus Prayer until Zacharia is finished. Then she kneels down while he places the lower part of his
priestly stole over her head and recites the words of absolution:
"May our Lord and God, Jesus Christ, by the grace and compassion of his love for man, pardon all your faults, child Zacharia,
and I, the unworthy priest _____, by his authority given me,
pardon and absolve you of all your sins: in the name of the Father
and of the Son and of the Holy Spirit."

With these last words, he traces the sign of the cross on the
head of this African woman who misses the liturgy only if ill.
Then Zacharia rises, turns to face him, and receives a final blessing before the next person comes forward and the confessions
continue.

Those in the line are men and women in approximately equal
numbers. They come in all ages and sizes, from children to the
aged. The only difference from the first confession is that in most
cases the priest understands the language being spoken and thus
can ask the occasional question and offer words of advice or encouragement before giving absolution.

There are those who whisper so quietly that probably the priest
can hardly hear them, others who speak so loudly that those standing nearby are likely to murmur aloud their own prayers so as not
to overhear what is being confessed. Some confess at length, some
briefly. Some confess with their hands hanging at their sides while
the hands of others articulate as much as words all that is being
said. Occasionally the penitent weeps more than speaks, confessing

mainly in tears. The sobs travel from one side of the church to the other and for some in the church prove contagious, one grief awakening others. With those whose pain is overwhelming, the priest often rests a reassuring hand on their shoulder.

Parents often bring infants and children with them when they confess. On a recent Sunday I noticed Fr. Sergei Ovsiannikov, rector of our parish, hearing a young mother's confession while holding her baby in his arms.

The frequency of confession varies dramatically from person to person. A few confess almost each week, some once a month, still others a few times in the course of a year. Only a small portion of the parish confesses on a given weekend. Even so, it is a big job for our priests. On Sunday mornings, one or two of them will be hearing confessions beginning about twenty minutes before the service begins, with one of them sometimes still hearing confessions through the first half of the liturgy, until it is nearly time for communion. It's not the ideal practice for confession to occur during the liturgy, but with many people coming long distances and sometimes experiencing delays along the way, the priests do their best to open the pathway to communion.

I'm sure I'm not the only one who feels a warm breeze entering the church from the corner where confessions are going on.

This is a scene repeated in Orthodox churches around the world, though details in practice vary from nation to nation. The Slavic wing of the Orthodox Church—our parish is linked to the Church in Russia—is noted for frequency of confession, the Greek wing less so, yet periodic confession is seen as an essential element of sacramental life even in those churches where it is less commonly used.

A Word of Thanks

Every book is a work of community. My thanks to all who read parts of the manuscript along the way and whose comments helped make it better, especially Barbara Allaire, Fr. Lawrence

Barriger, Fr. Ted Bobosh, Alice Carter, Tom Cornell, Fr. Yves
Dubois, Sr. Nonna Harrison, Ioana Novac, Fr. Sergei Ovsian-
nikov, Fr. Pat Reardon, Fr. Michael Plekon, Karen Rae Keck,
Shannon Robinson, Daniel Scuiry, Michael Sersch, Deacon John
Sewter, Fr. James Silver, Nilus Stryker, Sue Talley, Mary Taylor,
Fr. Steve Tsichlis, Fr. John Udies, Fr. Alexis Vinogradov, Bishop
Kallistos Ware, and Renee Zitzloff. I wish I could place a copy of
this book in the hands of the late Henri Nouwen, from whom I
learned a great deal about confession. He would be pleased to see
that Rembrandt's Prodigal Son painting graces the cover of this
book as it did one of his last books, *The Return of the Prodigal
Son*. Finally, a word of profound appreciation to my editor and
friend, Robert Ellsberg, and equally to my wife, Nancy. Without
them this book would never have reached your hands.

Hoping that one day there will be a revised edition of this book,
I invite any who read it to send me, care of the publisher or via e-
mail <alkmaar123@cs.com>, any suggestions, insights, or criti-
cisms with regard to this book and also to share stories or experiences of confession that might be useful to others. In the case of
private experiences of confession, names will not be published.
(Perhaps in the meantime some of these responses and corrections
can be posted on our web site—www.incommunion.org/home.htm.)

Jim Forest
Alkmaar, The Netherlands
The Feast of Sts. Peter and Paul, 2001

A THREE-LETTER WORD

Sin has always been an ugly word, but it has been made so in a new sense over the last half-century. It has been made not only ugly but passé. People are no longer sinful, they are only immature or underprivileged or frightened or, more particularly, sick.

—PHYLLIS MCGINLEY, *THE PROVINCE OF THE HEART*
"IN DEFENSE OF SIN"

What is failure? Failure is what people do ninety-nine percent of the time. Even in the movies: ninety-nine outtakes for one print. But in the movies they don't show the failures. What you see are the takes that work. So it looks as if every action, even going crazy, is carried off in a proper, rounded-off way. It looks as if real failure is unspeakable. TV has screwed up millions of people with their little rounded-off stories. Because that is not the way life is. Life is fits and starts, mostly fits.

—WALKER PERCY, *THE THANATOS SYNDROME*

There is no need to preach constantly on "sin," to judge and to condemn. It is when a man is challenged with the real contents of the Gospel, with its Divine depth and wisdom, beauty and all embracing meaning, that he becomes "capable of repentance," for true repentance is precisely the discovery by the man of the abyss that separates him from God and from His real offer to man. It is

1

when the man sees the bridal chamber adorned that he
realizes that he has no garment for entering it.
—FR. ALEXANDER SCHMEMANN[1]

A best-selling book of the 1970s had the title *I'm Okay, You're Okay*. One of its readers, a young priest in Boston, gave a sermon which was essentially a rave review. He wished he could give everyone a copy of the book. At the end of Mass, standing at the door, he asked one of his older parishioners if he had liked the sermon. The man responded, "I haven't read the book—maybe it's better than the Bible. But I kept thinking of Christ on the Cross saying to those who were watching him die, 'If everybody's okay, what in blazes am I doing up here?'"

The problem is I'm *not* okay and neither are you.

There have been thousands of essays and books in recent decades which have dealt with human failings under various labels without once using the one-syllable, three-letter word that has more bite than any of its synonyms: *sin*. Actions traditionally regarded as sinful have instead been seen as natural stages in the process of growing up, a result of bad parenting, a consequence of mental illness, an inevitable response to unjust social conditions, pathological behavior brought on by addiction, or even as "experiments in being." Sin, we've also been told, is an invention of repressed, hypocritical clerics who want to keep the rest of us in bondage—"priests in black robes binding with briars our joys and desires," in the chiming syllables of William Blake.

But what if I am more than a robot programmed by my past or my society or my economic status and actually can take a certain amount of credit—or blame—for my actions and inactions? Have I not done things I am deeply ashamed of, would not do again if I could go back in time, and would prefer no one to know about? What makes me so reluctant to call those actions "sins"? Is the word really out of date? Or is the problem that it has too sharp an edge?

The Hebrew verb *chata'*, "to sin," like the Greek word *hamartia*, literally means straying off the path, getting lost, missing the mark. Sin—going off course—can be intentional or unintentional. "You shoot an arrow, but it misses the target" a rabbi friend once explained to me. "Maybe it hits someone's backside, someone you didn't even know was there. You didn't mean it, but it's a sin. Or maybe you knew he was there—he was what you were aiming at. Then it's not a matter of poor aim but of hitting his backside intentionally. Now that's a sin!"

The Jewish approach to sin tends to be concrete. The author of the Book of Proverbs lists seven things which God hates:

> *A proud look, a lying tongue, hands that shed innocent blood, a heart that plots wicked deeds, feet that run swiftly to evil, a false witness that declares lies, and he that sows discord among the brethren.* (6:17-19)

As in so many other lists of sins, pride is given first place. "Pride goes before destruction, and a disdainful spirit before a fall" is another insight in the Book of Proverbs (16:18). In the Garden of Eden, Satan seeks to animate pride in his dialogue with Eve. Eat the forbidden fruit, he tells her, and "you will be like a god."

Pride is regarding oneself as god-like. In one of the stories preserved from early desert monasticism, a younger brother asks an elder, "What shall I do? I am tortured by pride." The elder responds, "You are right to be proud. Was it not you who made heaven and earth?" With those few words, the brother was cured of pride.

The craving to be ahead of others, to be more valued than others, to be more highly rewarded than others, to be able to keep others in a state of fear, the inability to admit mistakes or apologize—these are among the symptoms of pride. Pride opens the way for countless other sins: deceit, lies, theft, violence, and all those other actions that destroy community with God and with those around us.

"We're capable of doing some *rotten* things," the Minnesota storyteller Garrison Keillor notes, "and not all of these things are the result of poor communication. Some are the result of rottenness. People do bad, horrible things. They lie and they cheat and they corrupt the government. They poison the world around us. And when they're caught they don't feel remorse—they just go into treatment. They had a nutritional problem or something. They *explain* what they did—they don't feel bad about it. There's no guilt. There's just psychology."[2]

So eroded is our sense of sin that even in confession it often happens that people *explain* what they did rather than admit they did things that urgently need God's forgiveness. "When I recently happened to confess about fifty people in a typical Orthodox parish in Pennsylvania," the Orthodox theologian Fr. Alexander Schmemann wrote, "not one admitted to having committed any sin whatsoever!"[3]

For the person who has committed a serious sin, there are two vivid signs—the hope that what I did may never become known; and a gnawing sense of guilt. At least this is the case before the conscience becomes completely numb as patterns of sin become the structure of one's life to the extent that hell, far from being a possible next-life experience, is where I find myself in this life. (Rod Steiger in the film *The Pawnbroker*, in a desperate action to break free of numbness, slammed a nail-like spindle through his hand so he could finally feel something, even if it meant agonizing pain—a small crucifixion.)

It is a striking fact about our basic human architecture that we want certain actions to remain secret, not because of modesty but because there is an unarguable sense of having violated a law more basic than that in any law book—the "law written on our hearts" that St. Paul refers to (Rom 2:15). It isn't simply that we fear punishment. It is that we don't want to be thought of by others as a person who commits such deeds. One of the main obstacles to going to confession is dismay that someone else will know what I want no one to know.

Guilt is not quite the same thing.

Guilt is one of the themes of Walker Percy's *Love in the Ruins*. The central figure of the novel is Dr. Thomas More, a descendent of St. Thomas More, though the latest More is hanging

on to his faith by a frayed thread. He isn't likely to die a martyr
for the faith. Dr. More is both a physician and a patient at a
Louisiana mental hospital. From time to time he meets with his
colleague Max, a psychologist eager to cure More of guilt.

Max tells More,

> "We found out what the hangup was and we are get-
> ting ready to condition you out of it."
> "What hangup?"
> "Your guilt feelings."
> "I never did see that."

Max explains that More's guilt feelings have to do with adulterous sex.

> "Are you speaking of my fornication with Lola...?"
> asks More.
> "Fornication," repeats Max. "You see?"
> "See what?"
> "That you are saying that lovemaking is not a nat-
> ural activity, like eating and drinking."
> "No, I didn't say it wasn't natural."
> "But sinful and guilt-laden."
> "Not guilt-laden."
> "Then sinful?"
> "Only between persons not married to each other."
> "I am trying to see it as you see it."
> "I know you are."
> "If it is sinful, why are you doing it?"
> "It is a great pleasure."
> "I understand. Then, since it is 'sinful,' guilt feelings
> follow even though it is a pleasure."
> "No, they don't follow."
> "Then what worries you, if you don't feel guilty?"
> "That's what worries me: not feeling guilty."
> "Why does that worry you?"

"Because if I felt guilty, I could get rid of it."
"How?"
"By the sacrament of penance."
"I'm trying to see it as you see it."
"I know you are."[4]

Percy's novel reminds us that one of the oddest things about the age we live in is that we are made to feel guilty about feeling guilty. Dr. Thomas More is fighting against that. He may not yet experience guilt for his sins, but at least he knows that a sure symptom of moral death is *not* to feel guilty.

Dr. Thomas More—a modern man who can't quite buy the ideology that there are no sins and there is nothing to feel guilty about—is battling to recover a sense of guilt, which in turn will provide the essential foothold for contrition, which in turn can motivate confession and repentance. Without guilt, there is no remorse; without remorse there is no possibility of becoming free of habitual sins.

Yet there are forms of guilt that are dead-end streets. If I feel guilty that I have not managed to become the ideal person I occasionally want to be, or that I imagine others want me to be, then it is guilt that has no divine reference point. It is simply me contemplating me with the eye of an irritated theater critic. Christianity is not centered on performance, laws, principles, or the achievement of flawless behavior, but on Christ himself and participation in God's transforming love.

When Christ says, "Be perfect as your heavenly Father is perfect" (Mt 5:48), he is speaking not about the perfection of a student always obtaining the highest test scores or a child who manages not to step on any of the sidewalk's cracks, but of being whole, being in a state of communion, participating in God's love.

This is a condition of being that is suggested wordlessly by St. Andrei Rublev's icon of the Holy Trinity: those three angelic figures silently inclined toward each other around a chalice on a small altar. They symbolize the Holy Trinity: the communion that exists within God, not a closed communion restricted to them-

Icon of the Holy Trinity by Andrei Rublev

selves alone but an open communion of love in which we are not only invited but intended to participate.

A blessed guilt is the pain we feel when we realize we have cut ourselves off from that divine communion that radiates all creation. It is impossible not to stand on what Thomas Merton called "the hidden ground of love" but easy not to be aware of the hidden ground of love or even to resent it.

Like Dr. Thomas More, we may find ourselves hardly able to experience the guilt we know intellectually that we ought to feel not only for what we did, or failed to do, but for having fallen out of communion with God.

"Guilt," comments my Romanian friend Ioana Novac, "is a sense of fearful responsibility after realizing we have taken the wrong step and behold its painful consequences. In my experience, unfortunately not many people can tolerate this insight. My hunch is that many people these days experience less and less love, less and less strengthening support from their families and communities. As life gets more harried and we become more afflicted, the burden of guilt increases while our courage to embrace repentance—to look ourselves straight in the mirror and face the destructive consequences of our blindness and wrong choices—decreases."

It's a common delusion that one's sins are private or affect only a few other people. To think our sins, however hidden, don't affect others is like imagining that a stone thrown into the water won't generate ripples. As Bishop Kallistos Ware observed:

> *There are no entirely private sins. All sins are sins against my neighbor, as well as against God and against myself. Even my most secret thoughts are, in fact, making it more difficult for those around me to follow Christ.*[5]

This is a topic Garrison Keillor addressed in one of his Lake Wobegon stories.

A friend—Keillor calls him Jim Nordberg—writes a letter in which he recounts how close he came to committing adultery.

Nordberg describes himself waiting in front of his home for a colleague he works with to pick him up, a woman who seems to find him much more interesting and handsome than his wife does. They plan to drive to a professional conference in Chicago, though the conference isn't really what attracts Nordberg to this event. He knows what lies he has told others to disguise what he is doing. Yet his conscience hasn't stopped troubling him.

Sitting under a spruce tree, gazing up and down the street at all his neighbors' houses, he is suddenly struck by how much the quality of life in each house depends on the integrity of life next door, even if everyone takes everyone else for granted. "This street has been good for my flesh and blood," he says to himself. He is honest enough to realize that what he is doing could bring about the collapse of his marriage and wonders if in five or ten years his new partner might not tire of him and find someone else to take his place. It occurs to him that adultery is not much different from horse trading.

Again he contemplates his neighborhood:

> *As I sat on the lawn looking down the street, I saw that we all depend on each other. I saw that although I thought my sins could be secret, that they are no more secret than an earthquake. All these houses and all these families—my infidelity would somehow shake them. It will pollute the drinking water. It will make noxious gases come out of the ventilators in the elementary school. When we scream in senseless anger, blocks away a little girl we do not know spills a bowl of gravy all over a white table cloth. If I go to Chicago with this woman who is not my wife, somehow the school patrol will forget to guard the intersection and someone's child will be injured. A sixth grade teacher will think, "What the hell," and eliminate South America from geography. Our minister will decide, "What the hell—I'm not going to give that sermon on the poor." Somehow my adultery will cause the man in the grocery store to say, "To hell*

with the Health Department. This sausage was good yes-
terday—it certainly can't be any worse today." [6]

By the end of the letter it's clear that Nordberg decided not to go
to that conference in Chicago after all—a decision that was a moment of grace not only for him, his wife, and his children, but for
many others who would have been injured by his adultery.

"We depend on each other," Keillor says again, "more than
we can ever know."

Far from being hidden, each sin is another crack in the world.

One of the most widely used prayers, the Jesus Prayer, is
only one sentence long:

Lord Jesus Christ, Son of God, be merciful to me, a sinner!

Short as it is, many people drawn to it are put off by the last two
words. Those who teach the prayer are often asked, "But must I
call myself a sinner?" In fact that ending isn't essential, but our
difficulty using it reveals a lot. What makes me so reluctant to
speak of myself in such plain words? Don't I do a pretty good job
of hiding rather than revealing Christ in my life? Am I not a sinner? To admit that I am provides a starting point.

There are only two possible responses to sin: to justify it, or
to repent. Between these two there is no middle ground.

Justification may be verbal, but mainly it takes the form of
repetition: I do again and again the same thing as a way of
demonstrating to myself and others that it's not really a sin but
rather something normal or human or necessary or even good.
"After the first blush of sin comes indifference," wrote Henry
David Thoreau.[7] There is an even sharper Jewish proverb: "Commit a sin twice and it will not seem a crime."

Repentance, on the other hand, is the recognition that I cannot live any more as I have been living, because in living that
way I wall myself apart from others and from God. Repentance
is a change in direction. Repentance is the door of communion. It

is also a *sine qua non* of forgiveness. In the words of Fr. Alexander Schmemann, "There can be no absolution where there is no repentance."[8]

As St. John Chrysostom said sixteen centuries ago in Antioch:

Repentance opens the heavens, takes us to Paradise, overcomes the devil. Have you sinned? Do not despair! If you sin every day, then offer repentance every day! When there are rotten parts in old houses, we replace the parts with new ones, and we do not stop caring for the houses. In the same way, you should reason for yourself: if today you have defiled yourself with sin, immediately clean yourself with repentance.

FOUNDATIONS

Confession: The disclosing of something the knowledge of which by others is considered humiliating or prejudicial to the person confessing; a making known or acknowledging of one's fault, wrong, crime, weakness, etc. The acknowledging of sin or sinfulness. The confessing of sins to a priest; sacramental or auricular confession. Declaration of belief in or adhesion to; acknowledgment, profession, avowal when asked; specifically the testimony rendered by a Confessor.

—EXTRACTS FROM *THE OXFORD ENGLISH DICTIONARY*
SECOND EDITION

Confess yourself to heaven; repent what's past; avoid what is to come.

—WILLIAM SHAKESPEARE
HAMLET, ACT III, SCENE IV, LINE 149

Confession is a sacrament, a mystery. Divine grace is at work in it. Confession, like all the other sacraments, is God's action in which we, both penitent and priest, are invited to share.

—BISHOP KALLISTOS WARE

One of the yet-to-be-canonized saints of the last century, Dorothy Day, began her autobiography, *The Long Loneliness*, by describing going to confession on a Saturday night—entering the dimly lit vastness of the church, breathing in the smell of incense and candle wax, hearing the noise of the street seeping into the church as doors open and close, hearing the faint whispering as others confess their sins. Meanwhile there is the inner tumult of trying to recognize what needs to be confessed:

> *Going to confession is hard, hard when you have sins to confess, hard when you haven't, and you wrack your brain for even the beginnings of sins against charity, chastity, sins of distraction, sloth or gluttony. You do not want to make too much of your constant imperfections and venial sins, but you want to drag them out to the light of day as the first step in getting rid of them.... "I have sinned. These are my sins." That is all you are supposed to tell; not the sins of others, or your own virtues, but only your ugly, gray, drab, monotonous sins.[1]*

Dorothy wrote these reflections half a century ago. She was in her mid-fifties. In those days confession, most often on Saturday night, was a frequent practice in the Catholic Church. For Dorothy, as for many people, it was part of the basic geography of each week. Although confession has become less routine in recent years and confessionals have altogether vanished in many Catholic parishes, confession continues as a living sacrament in Catholic and Orthodox churches, with non-sacramental forms of it existing among Protestants.

While divisions that have occurred among Christians in the course of twenty centuries are all too evident in the various churches that have come into being through schism and sub-schism, with confession being one of the more damaged and controversial sacraments, all Christians still have in common the struggle to recognize sins by which we distance ourselves from God and from each other, to confess our sins at least in prayer if not to someone else, and to seek forgiveness both from God and from those who have been harmed by our sins. A Christian life is not possible without a dimension of grief for sins we have committed.

If much has changed in some sections of Christianity, what has not changed at all is the ongoing struggle described by Dorothy to see with clarity the failings of the most mysterious, most hidden being in the universe, myself. How much easier it is to announce the sins *other* people should confess!

Without confession, love is destroyed.

It is impossible to imagine a vital marriage or deep friendship without confession and forgiveness. If you have done something that damages a deep, loving relationship, confession is essential to its restoration. For the sake of that bond, you confess what you've done, you apologize, and you promise not to do it again.

In the context of religious life, confession is what we do to safeguard and renew our relationship with God whenever it is damaged. Confession restores our communion with God.

The purpose of confession is not to have one's sins dismissed as non-sins but to be forgiven and restored to communion. As the Evangelist John wrote: "If we confess our sins, he is faithful and just, and will forgive our sins and cleanse us from all unrighteousness" (1 Jn 1:9). The apostle James wrote in a similar vein: "Therefore confess your sins to one another, and pray for one another, that you may be healed" (Jas 5:16).

Confession is more than disclosure of sin. It also involves praise of God and profession of faith. Without the second and third elements, the first is pointless. To the extent we deny God, we reduce ourselves to accidental beings on a temporary planet in a random universe expanding into nowhere. To the extent we have a sense of the existence of God, we discover creation confessing God's being and see all beauty as a confession of God. "The world will be saved by beauty," Dostoevsky declared. We discover that faith is not so much something we *have* as something we *experience* —and we confess that experience much as glass confesses light. The Church calls certain saints "confessors" because they confessed their faith in periods of persecution even though they did not suffer martyrdom as a result. In dark, fear-ridden times, the faith shone through martyrs and confessors, giving courage to others.

In his autobiography, *Confessions*, Saint Augustine drew on all three senses of the word. He confessed certain sins, chiefly those that revealed the process that had brought him to baptism and made him a disciple of Christ and member of the Church. He confessed his faith. His book as a whole is a work of praise, a confession of God's love.

But it is the word's first meaning—confession of sins—that is usually the most difficult. It is never easy admitting to doing something you regret and are ashamed of, an act you attempted to keep secret or denied doing or tried to blame on someone else, perhaps arguing—to yourself as much as to others—that it wasn't actually a sin at all, or wasn't nearly as bad as some people might claim. In the hard labor of growing up, one of the most agonizing tasks is becoming capable of saying, "I'm sorry."

Yet we are designed for confession. Secrets in general are hard to keep, but unconfessed sins not only never go away but have a way of becoming heavier as time passes—the greater the sin, the heavier the burden. Confession is the only solution.

To understand confession in its sacramental sense, one first has to grapple with a few basic questions: Why is the Church involved in forgiving sins? Is priest-witnessed confession really needed? Why confess at all to any human being? In fact, why bother confessing to God even without a human witness? If God is really all-knowing, then he knows everything about me already. My sins are known before it even crosses my mind to confess them. Why bother telling God what God already knows?

Yes, truly God knows. My confession can never be as complete or revealing as God's knowledge of me and all that needs repairing in my life.

A related question we need to consider has to do with our basic design as social beings. Why am I so willing to connect with others in every other area of life, yet not in this? Why is it that I look so hard for excuses, even for theological rationales, not to confess? Why do I try so hard to explain away my sins until I've decided either they're not so bad or might even be seen as acts of virtue? Why is it that I find it so easy to *commit* sins yet am so reluctant, in the presence of another, to admit to having done so?

We are social beings. The individual as autonomous unit is a delusion. The Marlboro Man—the person without community, parents, spouse, or children—exists only on billboards. The *individual* is someone who has lost a sense of connection to others or attempts to exist in opposition to others—while the *person* exists in communion with other persons. At a conference of Orthodox Christians in France not long ago, in a discussion of the problem of individualism, a theologian confessed, "When I am in my car, I am an individual, but when I get out, I am a person again."

We are social beings. The language we speak connects us to those around us. The food I eat was grown by others. The skills passed on to me have slowly been developed in the course of hundreds of generations. The air I breathe and the water I drink is not for my exclusive use but has been in many bodies before mine. The place I live, the tools I use, and the paper I write on were made by many hands. I am not my own doctor or dentist or banker. To the extent I disconnect myself from others, I am in danger. Alone I die, and soon. To be in communion with others is life.

Because we are social beings, confession in church does not take the place of confession to those we have sinned against. An essential element of confession is doing all I can to set right what I did wrong. If I stole something, it must be returned or paid for. If I lied to anyone, I must tell that person the truth. If I was angry without good reason, I must apologize. I must seek forgiveness not only from God but from those whom I have wronged or harmed.

We are also verbal beings. Words provide not only a way of communicating with others but even with ourselves. The fact that confession is witnessed forces me to put into words all those ways, minor and major, in which I live as if there were no God and no commandment to love. A thought that is concealed has great power over us.

Confessing sins, or even temptations, makes us better able to resist. The underlying principle is described in one of the collections of sayings of the Desert Fathers, the Gerontikon:

> *If impure thoughts trouble you, do not hide them, but tell them at once to your spiritual father and condemn them. The more a person conceals his thoughts, the more they multiply and gain strength. But an evil thought, when revealed, is immediately destroyed. If you hide things, they have great power over you, but if you could only speak of them before God, in the presence of another, then they will often wither away, and lose their power.*

Confessing to anyone, even a bartender, taxicab driver, or stranger in an airport, renews rather than contracts my humanity, even if all I get in return for my confession is the well-worn remark, "Oh that's not so bad. After all, you're only human"— something like the *New Yorker* cartoon in which a psychologist reassures a Mafia contract killer stretched out on the couch, "Just because you do bad things doesn't mean you're bad."

But if I can confess to anyone anywhere, why confess in church in the presence of a priest? It's not a small question in societies in which the phrase "institutionalized religion" is so often used, the implicit message being that religious institutions necessarily impede or undermine religious life. Yet it's not a term we seem inclined to adapt to other contexts. Few people would prefer we got rid of institutionalized health care or envision a world without institutionalized transportation. Whatever we do that involves more than a few people requires structures.

Confession is a Christian ritual with a communal character. Confession in the church differs from confession in your living room in the same way that getting married in church differs from simply living together. The communal aspect of the event tends to safeguard it, solidify it, and call everyone to account—those doing the ritual, and those witnessing it.

In the social structure of the Church, a huge network of local communities is held together in unity, each community helping the others and all sharing a common task while each provides a specific place to recognize and bless the main events in life from birth to burial. Confession is an essential part of that continuum. My confession is an act of reconnection with God and with all the people and creatures who depend on me and have been harmed by my failings and from whom I have distanced myself through acts of non-communion. The community is represented by the person hearing my confession, an ordained priest delegated to serve as Christ's witness, who provides guidance and wisdom that helps each penitent overcome attitudes and habits that take us off course, who declares forgiveness and restores us to communion. In this way our repentance is brought into the community that has been damaged by our sins—a private event in a public context.

"It's a fact," writes Orthodox theologian Fr. Thomas Hopko, rector of St. Vladimir's Seminary, "that we cannot see the true ugliness and hideousness of our sins until we see them in the mind and heart of the other to whom we have confessed."[2]

A SHORT HISTORY
OF CONFESSION

If there is symbol of confession in the West, it is the closet-like structure known as the confessional. Anyone who has seen such movies as *Moonstruck, I Love You to Death,* or *Angela's Ashes* has had a vicarious experience of being inside a confessional and can recall how the Catholic penitent traditionally begins with the words, "Bless me, Father, for I have sinned. It has been ____ weeks (or months or years) since my last confession."

While the confessional gives the impression of having been there forever, in fact it wasn't there for three-quarters of Christian history and has never been taken up in the East. It was an innovation introduced by Saint Charles Borromeo, one of the eminent figures of the Counter-Reformation, when he was archbishop of Milan. In 1577 his staff published a set of diocesan rules for church architecture that for the first time described the confessional. It was to be a wooden structure of three vertical panels enclosing a seat to be used by the priest, a door in front of the priest's stall, and a kneeling bench for the penitent's use on one side (a later design would put kneeling benches on both sides of the priest). Between priest and penitent was a small window divided by two thin wooden columns, covered on the priest's side with a thin cloth and on the penitent's side with a perforated metal sheet. The confessional was to stand in an open and visible part of the church, normally the nave, oriented in such a way that the penitent was kneeling in the direction of the altar.

The new structure spread rapidly in the West. By 1614, thirty years after Borromeo's death, the design was incorporated into the Vatican's *Rituale Romanum* and before the end of the century confessionals were found in every Catholic church.

The structure was new but confession was otherwise unchanged. One can see the earlier Western practice in a painting of the seven sacraments made in 1441 by the Flemish artist Rogier van der Weyden.[1] In it we see a priest with a hood-like piece of grey fabric draped over his head. He is sitting in a chair, his back toward an altar where Mass is being celebrated, and his right hand rests on the head of a penitent kneeling before him, a white-haired man whose hat is placed on the floor by his knees. With his left hand the priest is making a gesture of encouragement; his inclined face is attentive and sympathetic. Nearby a kneeling woman waits her turn, her hands pressed together in prayer.

It is a scene similar to what one still finds in the Orthodox Church. For many centuries the unchanged Orthodox custom has been for priest and penitent to stand (in some cases to sit) side-by-side before an icon of Christ near the sanctuary, the area of the church that surrounds the altar. The icon is lit by a votive lamp or candle. Beneath the icon is a small table on which are placed a New Testament and a cross. The penitent faces the icon of Christ, which serves as a reminder that it is Christ who hears the confession and Christ who forgives; the priest is there chiefly as a witness.[2]

Confession—the sacrament of repentance and reconciliation —has been part of Christian life from the early days of the Church, though details of confessional practice are mentioned only briefly in texts surviving from the first three centuries. Saint Matthew notes that as people came to be baptized by John in the Jordan they confessed their sins (Mt 3:6). The foundational sacrament of baptism, the rite of entrance into the Church, has always been linked with repentance. "Repent, and be baptized...in the name of Jesus Christ for the forgiveness of your sins," Saint Peter preached in Jerusalem, "and you shall receive the gift of the Holy Spirit" (Acts 2:38).

*Detail of "The Seven Sacraments" by Rogier van der Weyden
depicting confession in a medieval church*

The development of the theology of confession and the rites through which sinners were reconciled to the Church was a gradual process. Time and again the issue of forgiveness and the penitent's return to sacramental life within the Church became a matter of white-hot controversy.

In the first generations of Christianity, conversion was so momentous an event, the community of believers so small, motivation so profound, and preparation for baptism so thorough, that it came as a shock to the community that any member, once baptized, would ever again commit a serious sin. During the catechumen's prolonged preparation for baptism, past sins were confessed and acknowledged and a path of determined repentance followed. Conversion meant a basic change in attitude and direction, a renewal of life, root, and branch. No one would choose baptism lightly nor imagine that the rest of one's life would be as it was before. It was no exaggeration to speak of the Church as a community of saints—a people who had given up everything that impeded life in the kingdom of God.

In catechetical texts that have survived from the first three centuries, we see how clearly expressed were the Church's behavioral expectations in every area of life. Conversion to Christ meant a lifelong commitment to bear witness to Christ and his resurrection in every word and action. Truly a second birth, baptism offered a once-in-a-lifetime fresh start and at the same time made each person co-responsible for preserving the holiness of the Church. In an age of martyrs and confessors, living among a reborn, forgiven people, well formed in their faith, deeply motivated and often residing in close-knit communities, grave sins—murder, abortion, adultery, and apostasy—were far less likely to occur than in a Church made up of hundreds of thousands of people whose conversion was at least in part an act of social conformity.

A well-defined ritual of sacramental confession as it now exists in the Church had not yet emerged. Minor sins, it was held, were redeemed through prayer, works of mercy, and the reception of communion. But we can see in the letter of the apostle James that confession was an integral part of Christian life: "Confess your sins to one another" (Jas 5:16). A passage in the writings of the North African theologian, Tertullian, gives us a glimpse of confession of sins as it was practiced in the Church at the end of the second century:

Prostrate yourself at the feet of the priests and kneel before the beloved of God, thus making all the brethren commissioned ambassadors of your prayer for pardon.[3]

In the early years of the third century, Origen of Alexandria listed seven ways of obtaining forgiveness:

First, we are baptized for the remission of sins. Second, there is the suffering of martyrdom. Third, there is the remission of sins given in return for works of mercy. Fourth, we obtain forgiveness through our forgiveness of others. Fifth, forgiveness is won when a man has converted a sinner from the error of his ways. Sixth, sins are remitted through an abundance of love. Finally there is a seventh way of forgiveness, hard and painful though it is, namely remission of sins through penitence, when the sinner washes his bed with tears, and tears are his bread day and night, and when he does not hold back in shame from declaring his sin to the priest of the Lord and asking for medicine.[4]

The seventh way was especially for those who had committed offenses that would later be called "deadly" sins. Grave sins were confessed in public to the church community, with the local bishop present, or the bishop (or a priest he had delegated) would meet privately with the person who had lost his way, trying to help him realize that his action was a serious sin. The bishop then notified the local church that the person was undergoing penance and was forbidden to receive the Eucharist until formally forgiven and reconciled. This provided the baptized with a second chance to live up to their baptismal commitments—a "plank after shipwreck."

For the unrepentant, the Church's last resort was excommunication: exclusion and shunning. It appears to have been rare but it certainly happened. Paul had written about excommunication to the young church in Corinth:

> *When you are assembled, and my spirit is present, with the power of our Lord Jesus, you are to deliver this man to Satan for the destruction of the flesh, that his spirit may be saved on the day of the Lord Jesus.* (1 Cor 5:4-5)

Excommunication was not intended as punishment but rather to inspire repentance. Apparently the measure bore fruit in this particular instance. In his second letter to the Corinthians, Paul wrote:

> *For such a one this punishment by the majority is enough; so you should rather turn to forgive and comfort him, or he may be overwhelmed by excessive sorrow. So I beg you to reaffirm your love for him.* (2 Cor 2:6-8)

Despite periodic waves of repression, the Church grew steadily until by the end of the third century it had become a conspicuous part of society throughout the Roman Empire. But so large a Christian population inevitably included many with a more superficial commitment. Increasingly there were Christians who were little troubled by long-standing social norms and who preferred to honor martyrs rather than emulate them. Periods of persecution revealed that fear of arrest, the possibility of torture and execution, could drive some who had been baptized to offer sacrifice to idols or sign declarations that might spare them and their families from punishment. Yet many who had saved themselves from the possibility of dispossession, torture, or martyrdom afterward regretted their weakness and returned in remorse to the Church, begging forgiveness and readmittance.

Among the significant controversies dividing Christians in these formative years was the question as to whether it could forgive and receive apostates back into the Church and, if so, how to do this and what sort of penance to require of those who returned.

Callistus, Bishop of Rome from 217 until 222, took a lenient approach toward those who sought readmittance, citing the parables of the lost sheep and the prodigal son as proof that no sin is unforgivable and that the Church is called to extend God's mercy to any who seek it, no matter how grave their sins. He was not without opponents, among them the priest Novatian.

When contention divided the Christian community in Rome in 251 over who should be the next bishop, Cornelius—a supporter of Callistus's forgiving approach—was chosen over Novatian. Those who opposed the readmittance of baptized Christians who had compromised themselves during periods of persecution set up a counter-church led by Novatian. During the Valerian persecution seven years later, Novatian himself was martyred, but Novatianists spread into Gaul and Spain. The split lasted until the seventh century.

In North Africa in the middle of the third century, Cyprian, bishop of Carthage, was one of those to expound on the Church's duty to forgive those who embraced *exomologesis*—a Greek word meaning confession, both of faith and of sins, joined with publicly manifested repentance.

Cyprian also gives us a glimpse of the ritual of forgiveness and reconciliation that already existed in the Church: the laying of hands on the head or shoulders on the penitent, a gesture still used at the end of confession in the Orthodox Church and once again in use in the Catholic Church. This simple, intimate action signifies healing and the restoration of communion. Interestingly, one also finds accounts of the gesture in reverse—the penitent laying his hands on the shoulders of the priest: a sign of the priest accepting the burden for all that was confessed to him.

This sacramental gesture was already being used in the first century. There is a passage in Paul's letter to Timothy in which he advises: "Do not be hasty in the laying on of hands, nor participate in another man's sins; keep yourself pure" (1 Tim 5:22). Today some read this as an admonition to take great care before ordaining a man to the priesthood, but the text can also be understood as a caution not to forgive unless there is certainty that the person being forgiven truly repents of his sins—otherwise the priest makes himself a party to sin rather than an absolver. In either case, it's clear that the laying on of hands was an element of Christian sacramental life from the beginning.

What was new in third-century Christian practice was the creation of a canonical Order of Penitents within the Church: men and women who had committed serious sins embracing a period of penance and instruction in preparation for reconciliation with the community of Christ's disciples. The Church had dismissed as heresy the idea that the gravest sins could be forgiven only, if ever, by God after death, but it chose to make the return to the eucharistic community a demanding process.

For example, the Canons of Hippolytus, written in Rome before 233, state: "If anyone has shed [human] blood, let him not take part in the [eucharistic] mysteries, unless he has been purified by a punishment, by tears and groans." Depending on the sin, varying periods of time of exclusion from the Eucharist were assigned—three to seven years were not uncommon.

The *Didaskalia*, written in Syria in the same period, describes a well-developed penitential system in which the laying on of hands is used both as a sign of reception into the community of penitents—"the making of a penitent"—and later as a sign of forgiveness.

In the Syrian Church the usual period of penance was much shorter than in the West: weeks rather than years. "The churches of the East not only seem more lenient," comments the Catholic scholar, James Dallen, in his study of the history of sacramental confession, "but also more able to have a public discipline without embarrassing and discouraging penitents. The Eastern emphasis on spiritual direction, the healing function of the Church's ministers, and private counsel as a way of entering formal penance as well as a way of dealing with [lesser] sins not subject to that discipline, all contributed to the ease with which the Eastern Church passed from public ecclesial penance to private sacramental penance without losing an ecclesial sense."[5]

It was a situation in which penance, confession, and forgiveness would play a more and more important role in Christian life.

What did penance involve? The central elements were increased prayer, fasting, and almsgiving, with more time devoted to the needs of the poor. Plain clothing was put on, such as might be worn by a person in mourning. Like catechumens, penitents attended only the first half of the liturgy during which the scriptures were read and the sermon was given. Before the eucharistic liturgy began, catechumens and penitents were dismissed after being prayed for and blessed. Finally, when the prescribed time had passed and it was clear that contrition was genuine, in the midst of the liturgy the penitent would be exhorted not to sin again. Forgiveness would then be declared with the laying on of hands by the bishop.

In 303 the emperor Diocletian launched Rome's last major assault on Christians. Though intended by Diocletian to take a milder form—Christians were to be stripped of citizenship and the right to own property—his edicts occasioned not only dispossession but widespread torture and killing of Christ's followers.

The brutality unleashed during Diocletian's reign also engendered a schism within the Church on the southern edge of the Mediterranean. When Caecilian was consecrated bishop in Carthage, some argued that his consecration was invalid because it had been done by a bishop who, it was charged, had surrendered sacred texts to the police for burning, and thus was a traitor. (The word traitor has its roots in the Latin verb *tradere*, to deliver or hand over.) A rival bishop was elected, splitting the local church. He in turn was succeeded by Donatus, who fervently preached against pardoning those who had failed the test when faced with persecution. He also argued that the ordination of priests and consecration of bishops was invalid if the person performing the ordination was unworthy. These early Puritans became known as Donatists. It proved a long-lasting schism with thousands of parish communities and, at its height, five hundred bishops. (At this time bishops were responsible for much smaller geographic areas—not counting Donatist hierarchs, there were seven hundred bishops in North Africa alone in Augustine's era.)

In the fourth century, with Christians finding themselves no longer a target of persecution but members of the religion the emperor most respected and favored, a borderline was crossed. If before there had been many who were more well adjusted to the world than should be the case among Christ's followers, now they became the majority. "The Church after Constantine ceased to be a minority of heroically minded 'faithful,'" the Orthodox theologian Fr. Alexander Schmemann has written. "She identified herself almost completely with the 'world'... and had to deal with a multitude of nominal Christians in need of help, constant guidance and personal care."[6]

Augustine (354–430) grew up in the midst of a North African society that was largely Christian but was bitterly divided between Catholics and Donatists. Among the Donatists were club-wielding men who dubbed themselves the Lord's Athletes and called their weapons "Israels." They regarded themselves as ordained by God to attack "the unworthy" should they dare approach a martyr's shrine. On occasion they beat the unworthy to death. Division was so deep that Donatist bakers would refuse to sell bread to non-Donatists.

As a bishop, Augustine became one of the most formidable opponents of Donatist heresy, though also their protector when the governor sentenced Donatists to death. "We should prefer to see them released," he told the governor, "rather than avenge our brother's murder by further bloodshed."[7] He opposed capital punishment because, as he pointed out to the governor, only a living person could undertake soul-saving penance.

The readiness to forgive and be reconciled with those who sought forgiveness and gave a clear sign of repentance was one of the hallmarks of orthodox (from the Greek for right believing or right praising) and catholic (universal, as opposed to sectarian) Christianity. Among the traits of heretical sects was an unwillingness to forgive those who failed to meet the groups' standards of behavior.

By the fifth century, with Christianity the dominant religion of the Roman Empire, prolonged instruction of those who would be baptized was rare, as the candidates were now mainly infants or children. Where there were adult converts, they were prepared for baptism in a matter of weeks—during Lent—rather than months or years as in earlier times. By this time, the Order of Penitents began to fill a need that in the first several centuries had been met by rigorous preparation for baptism. The Order of Penitents acquired a semi-monastic character to the extent that to become a penitent was often described as "assuming the habit"—that is, wearing plain clothing—the same phrase that would later be used for those entering the monastery.

A text written by Sozomen in Rome about 450 describes entrance into the Order of Penitents:

> *[There is an area of the Church] in which spot they stand and mourn until the completion of the services, for it is not lawful for them to take part in the [eucharistic] mysteries; then they cast themselves, with groans and lamentations, prostrate on the ground. The bishop conducts the ceremony, sheds tears, and prostrates himself in like manner; after this all the people burst into tears and groan aloud. Afterwards the bishop rises from the ground and raises up the others, then offers up prayer on behalf of the penitents and dismisses them. Each of the penitents subjects himself in private to voluntary suffering [by fasting and refraining from baths] until a certain period set by the bishop has passed. When the time arrives, he is made free from the consequences of his sin and assembles in the Church with the people.*[8]

Lent—originally a season of final preparation for baptism—gradually evolved into a period of penitential activity for all Christians, with particular stress on increased almsgiving, strict fasting, and confession before Easter, still the custom in much of the Orthodox Church as well as in some portions of the Catholic Church. Instead of some entering the Order of Penitents, by the seventh century the whole Church followed the way of penance together for the six weeks preceding Pascha. Wednesdays and Fridays throughout most of the year also became days of collective penitential fasting.

When we think of confession, most of us think of it as among life's most private experiences and assume that private confession of sins was always the norm in Christianity. But in the early centuries confession (meaning confession of grave sin) was as public as the liturgy. It was only in 459 that Pope Leo I did away with the requirement that penitents read out a list of their sins to the whole congregation.

In monasteries, however, a model of private confession was beginning to emerge.

Monasticism was itself something new. When the age of persecution ended in the fourth century, the deserts of Egypt, Palestine, Arabia, and Persia were invaded by men and women intent on finding the gateway to the kingdom of God in regions where they would be tested by a harsh environment, live from hard labor (many supported themselves as basket weavers), and experience a bare minimum of social life. Some were hermits; most lived in communities. In an earlier time these self-made outcasts would have been the ones most likely to be arrested for their faith, but now Christians were praised and rewarded rather than persecuted. The biographies of Saints Paul and Anthony, the first of the "desert fathers," are among the most influential books ever written. Many were inspired to join communities of prayer in barren places while others embraced a more ascetic life in towns and cities.

What we know of the desert fathers (and that much rarer breed, the desert mothers, such as Saint Mary of Egypt, a former prostitute from Alexandria who ended her life in the Judean wilderness) has come down to us chiefly in collections of sayings of the elders and brief stories about them.

There is, for example, Abba Moses the Black, who was a robber before he became a monk. Summoned to a community meeting at which a certain brother was to be condemned for his faults, he arrived dragging behind him an old basket from which sand was pouring out through several holes. When he was asked why he was doing this, he replied, "My sins are running out behind me and I do not see them and today I come to judge another!" His gesture inspired the brothers to pardon the one accused.

Though words were at times connected with dramatic actions, more often all we are given are sayings from the elders—perhaps a single sentence spoken in reply to the request, "Give us a word." Such "words" were spoken by men who were renowned for their silence, providing a kind of spiritual manna that supplemented sacred scripture. The monastic elders stressed conversion, compassion, and forgiveness, which they saw as far more important than the most extreme ascetic practices. As one elder declared, "If a man have humility and poverty and judge not another, that is how the fear of the Lord gets into him." Another elder taught, "It is better to eat meat and drink wine than by detraction to devour the flesh of your brother."[9]

One of the innovations that developed in monastic communities was private confession to an older monk who became one's spiritual father. Those not so far along in the spiritual life turned for guidance to elders who were closer to the kingdom of God, opening their hearts to them. Bishop Kallistos Ware comments:

In the practice of such spiritual counsel, the scope is far wider than in the formal penance of the Church. What you disclose to your elder is not just your sins, but your thoughts. You don't just speak of what you've done wrong, you share with him your inner state, your whole situation. The hope is that by revealing your thoughts to your elder, you will in fact avoid falling into sin. In other words, penance is retrospective, picking up the pieces after the breakage; but, through the use of spiritual counsel, you hope to avoid the breakage itself.[10]

The younger monk asks the elder for advice and also for some reassurance of God's forgiveness. This had always been a spontaneous dimension of life in the Church, but in communities of monks the practice began to acquire a more formal character. In his life of prayer and listening, the monk became painfully aware of how easily he could deceive himself and what a poor judge he was of his own behavior. Aware of the many ways in which he fell short of what God had created him to be, he realized with urgency his need for God's forgiveness yet could hardly believe himself worthy of it. But the word of someone we know is close to God becomes a word from God uttered through that person's lips. It is not hard to imagine how an elder must often have said to a weeping young monk who felt he was beyond God's forgiveness, "Our God is mercy. It is because of his mercy that you have told me these things. God has been listening—I am only a witness—but I can assure you God forgives you."

While originally only a monastic practice, little by little the custom of private confession spread to the wider Church, losing in the process something of its communal monastic character. There was a constant stream of visitors seeking help and assurance of God's pardon who appealed to monastic elders to hear their confessions, to assist them with questions that were troubling them, and to give them counsel and direction. In time, not only monks but also respected local priests—and possibly saintly deacons and lay people—were sought out by those wishing to confess their sins, seek counsel, and be assured of God's forgiveness.

Among monks in the East, the understanding of confession was essentially medicinal, an attitude that persists in the Orthodox Church today. Sin was seen as illness. If a particular penance was suggested, it was to help heal the soul. The cure for a spiritual disease was not a penalty but rather an embracing of the opposite of the disease. Hatred is cured not by chastisements but by learning to pray for the person hated, which in turn opens the way to love.

As monasticism spread, the "desert" became any harsh, unlikely place. Monks could be found not only in the deserts of

Egypt but also on storm-battered rocks jutting out of the Atlantic off the west coast of Ireland at what seemed the world's end. By the end of the fifth century, thanks chiefly to Saint Patrick's missionary labors, Christian belief had spread throughout Ireland, assuming there a distinctly Celtic character. In place of a town- or city-centered church, monastic communities were the focal points of Irish religious life. The most influential figures were abbots and abbesses, who often overshadowed bishops. Far from being cut off, monastic life was intertwined with lay life and provided a pattern for life on farms and in villages.

As in the East, private confession was an aspect of Irish monastic life, and here too gradually became part of the common practice of the local church as a whole, though Celtic culture gave confession a different character than it had in the East. There was a deeply imbedded conviction among Celts that every crime had to be paid for—not in vengeance but in ways that restored social balance. If someone stole a cow, there was a certain penalty, and still another for an injury or death. Normally this involved payment or doing labor on behalf of those one had harmed. Celtic tradition had established a wide range of penalties specific to every possible offense.

When the Irish were converted, sin was seen simply as another word for crime. It was obvious to Celtic Christians that each sin, like each crime, must have its particular penalty—God might be merciful but one could not gain that mercy cheaply. It had to be won by difficult deeds. In the case of lesser sins, the penalties began with prayer and fasting, then went on to acts of penance such as kneeling on a stone for a set period or praying with outstretched arms. In extreme cases involving the gravest sins, the penalty could be exile, as was the case for Saint Columba after he—a young prince who had become a monk—regarded himself as bearing part of the guilt for a battle in which many died. "Ill have I served the heavenly kingdom," he confessed, "and ill have I served Ireland in that I have caused the men of Ireland to shed one another's blood. Men lie dead through the pride of a man of peace."

In penance, Columba went to Iona in the Inner Hebrides on the western edge of Scotland, vowing that he would not rest until he had converted as many men as had died in the battle. In time this remote island became one of the principal centers of Christian life and missionary activity. The famous Gospel text, *The Book of Kells*, the crowning work of Celtic art, was very likely made on Iona. Queens and kings, among them Macbeth, were buried next to the abbey church. In northwest Europe, Iona was regarded as second only to Jerusalem as a blessed place to await the general resurrection when Christ will judge the living and the dead.

The Irish had come to their faith through missionaries and, from the end of the sixth century, were to become missionaries second to none, traveling to every part of Europe and even as far to the east as Russia. (In 1987 I happened to be present when an Irish standing cross was unearthed beneath the floor of Russia's most ancient church, Holy Wisdom Cathedral in Novgorod, startling evidence of Irish influence in Russia more than a thousand years ago. The cathedral's bronze doors are not only beautiful works of art but unique in another respect, each relief icon being identified on one side in the Cyrillic alphabet, on the other in Latin. When Eastern and Western Christians at last bridge their differences, perhaps the ideal location to celebrate the event would be Holy Wisdom Cathedral in Novgorod.)

Traveling with the Irish monks was their practice and understanding of confession and repentance. This left an enduring mark wherever they went, helping shape the character of sacramental confession in the West.

Not all the clergy were pleased with the more private approach to penance that the monks introduced. The new methods were especially suspect because they depended only indirectly on the local bishop. Though the old system with its Order of Penitents hardly functioned anymore, the principle still existed. An attempt was made to revive the old form of canonical penance. In France, local church councils—at Tours and Rheims in 813 and in Paris in 829—criticized the Irish practice, which was seen as encouraging laxity and lacking the traditional public dimension.

Books (called penitentials) with guidelines for those hearing confessions were condemned. The council in Paris went so far as to order the burning of such books.

Despite these rulings, the method introduced by Irish monastics met a need so urgent for so many people that the practice could not be suppressed. Church councils responded by turning from blanket condemnation to conditional acceptance, requiring only that private confession of sins be limited to those actions not subject to canonical discipline. The principle was public penance for public sins, private penance for private sins.[11]

In theory, serious crimes of a public character would result in excommunication with a return to the sacraments allowed only after a period of public penance that ended with the bishop personally presiding at a public ritual of reconciliation. In practice, attempts at renewing the old method had little impact. Shortly before his death in 840, Jonas of Orléans described canonical penance as "rare in the Church today."[12] Yet there was a marked increase in such private penitential practices as going on pilgrimage to holy places.

What had been originally a spontaneous response by monks to the spiritual needs of lay people at last became part of ordinary Christian life, finally including a formal act of forgiveness and reconciliation to eucharistic life, though—except for those close to death—normally forgiveness did not occur until the completion of whatever penance had been assigned.

A text written about 817 has survived which gives a clear account of the practice of confession at the time. The confessor (a priest, though a deacon could restore a penitent to communion in emergency situations) was advised to fast with the penitent for at least one day. The confessor was expected to be a person of prayer, seeking God's mercy for himself and the penitent. He was to advise the penitent and assign a penance—a period of fasting, unless other actions were more appropriate: ransoming captives, making donations to the poor, or serving at the altar. The confessor was urged to be especially compassionate and lenient with the poor and with servants. After reciting several psalms, the confes-

sor would lay his hands on the penitent and recite a prayer for forgiveness. The penitent completed the process during Holy Week
when the bishop would confirm his reconciliation.[13]

A century later, in 950, a similar text proposed that the confessor ask the penitent if he knew the Our Father and question
him about the Creed: belief in the Holy Trinity, the resurrection
and the Last Judgment, and readiness to forgive others. Then the
penitent was to be asked, "Do you believe that through confession
and sincere correction your sins are forgiven by God?" After a
positive response, penance was given and both priest and penitent
prayed together. The priest was advised to take the penitent's abil-
ities into account and not to assign too heavy a penance.[14]

In another text found in the Romano-Germanic Pontifical, the
confessor is counseled: "Warn [the penitent] not to despair. God
is merciful and forgives all sins if one only reforms.... The person who becomes the child of the devil by sinning can become
the child of God again by doing penance. The one who ought to
go to hell can instead enter paradise."[15]

Penance was more than a rosary or a few Our Fathers to be
recited. Those guilty of serious sins might be required to spend all
of Lent in a monastery. Others might be sent on an arduous and
often dangerous pilgrimage to a holy shrine.

By the turn of the first millennium, private confession had
become deeply embedded in the life of the Church. Private confession, far from being the suspect practice it had once been, became an ordinary aspect of Christian life. No longer were penitents excluded from the eucharistic liturgy but only from
reception of the sacrament until their reconciliation was complete.

Beginning in the tenth century, another custom took root in
the West: the placing of ashes on the forehead of those entering a
period of penance—the genesis of Ash Wednesday at the beginning of Lent.

In the era of canonical penance, formal confession had im-
plied the commission of a grave sin. Gradually every failure to
follow the way of Christ or the regulations of the Church (such as
attending the liturgy every Sunday and major feast day and keep-

ing the fasts) became a matter for confession, with a formal distinction made by theologians in the West between venial (lesser, from *venia*, forgiveness) and mortal (capital or deadly) sins.

Priests sought ways to cope with all those who felt burdened by their sins, many of which were minor. From the ninth to the fourteenth centuries, one solution was the development of a penitential liturgy supplementing private confession—readings followed by communal confession of lesser sins and then an absolution pronounced collectively. Scholastic theologians would later regard such general confessions as "sacramentals"—actions potentially having the significance of receiving a sacrament, in this case depending not on the rite itself but the sincerity of the person.

By the beginning of the twelfth century, confession and absolution had normally become part of the same event, without a period of penance or acts of restitution being imposed between the two, though a penance of some kind would still be assigned. Only certain grave sins had to be referred to the local bishop for absolution.

In the year 1215, it was decided by the bishops at the Fourth Lateran Council in Rome that all who had attained the "age of reason" should confess at least once a year, prior to Easter.[16]

Mirroring changes in penitential and confessional practices were developments in religious art. Early Christian images of Christ's crucifixion stressed the voluntary nature of his suffering and the motivation of self-giving love. The large crucifix before which Saint Francis of Assisi heard Christ's voice in 1206 is an excellent example of the Byzantine iconographic tradition in which the stress is less on Christ's suffering than on his voluntary gift of himself "for the life of the world"—a phrase used in the Orthodox liturgy. But the cross before which Francis prayed was already old, probably made two centuries earlier. Western religious art of the thirteenth century had begun to stress the torture that Christ endured step by step from the Garden of Gethsemane until the moment he gave up his spirit at the Place of the Skull. Such images reflected a movement of devotionalism in which the individual becomes ever more deeply aware of how his own sins

The "Assisi Cross"

add to Christ's suffering—"not only did he die *for* me, but *because* of me and my sins."

By the late medieval period, with communion of lay people occurring only rarely, confession had become the *essential* sacrament. "Individual confession and absolution had become the primary, if not the only, symbol of post-baptismal conversion," James Dallen remarks.[17]

The tragic Great Schism dividing Christianity along East-West lines had happened in 1054, when three legates from Rome placed a Bull of Excommunication on the main altar of the Hagia Sophia—Holy Wisdom—Cathedral in Constantinople.[18] Christianity in the East was to change very little in the millennium that followed. An eleventh-century Christian, were he transported into an Orthodox Church of the present day, would be more surprised at changes in lighting and heating than in religious rites or the climate of worship. But in the sixteenth century, Christendom in the West began to splinter along both national and theological lines. One result was that the practice of sacramental confession was to survive in the West only in the Catholic Church.

Not all reformers sought such a result. Martin Luther did not attack confession as such but rather the Catholic system of indulgences.[19] The sale of indulgences in Germany as a way of raising money for a new Saint Peter's Basilica in Rome outraged Luther and led him to challenge the concept of indulgences and not merely their sale. Luther did not oppose the sacrament of penance as such but regarded it as valid only insofar as it revealed God's grace and encouraged the sinner to trust fully in God's mercy. He especially objected to the detailed cataloging of all past sins in confession, which he saw as a torment to the penitent, an irritant to the confessor, and a waste of time for both—as well as an implicit indication of lack of confidence in God's mercy.

While Luther did not altogether reject sacramental confession, there were other reformers who did, though some forms of it are occasionally found in Protestant—most notably Pentecostal—churches today. In 1987, I was present at a Christmas service in a large Baptist Church in Kiev during which a young woman pub-

licly confessed a grave sin she had committed and was readmitted
to the congregation.[20]

The Catholic Church responded to the Reformation with its
own reform, the main guidelines of which were laid down by the
Council of Trent (1545–63). By the end of the sixteenth century,
many of the abuses that had sparked the Reformation had been
eliminated, but division among Christians in the West had grown
far wider and deeper than reformers like Luther had ever envi-
sioned. The martyr-scarred schism had passed beyond forgiveness
and healing. Even today, one occasionally smells the bitter smoke
of that era.

The response of the Council of Trent to controversy regarding confession was to insist that Christ had given the Church the
responsibility of binding and loosing sins and that therefore confession, far from being a Church invention, was implanted in the
Gospel as well as in tradition. Christ obliged his followers to forgive sins and repeatedly gave a personal example of doing so.
While all Christians were required to forgive, it was an essential
element of priestly ministry to hear confessions, to encourage renewed conversion, to guide penance, and to reconcile to the
Church those who sincerely repented, assuring them of God's forgiveness. Thus the opportunity had to exist within every parish
for sins to be privately confessed and absolution given, so long as
the priest hearing the confession was convinced that the penitent's
intention to overcome sin in his or her life was genuine.

One dimension of the Council's work was to deepen the ecclesial understanding of confession—that it had to do not only
with the individual, seen in isolation, but with his life in the eucharistic community of the Church.

While recognizing confession as one of seven sacraments
which Christ had intended for the Church as means of salvation,
the Council also acknowledged that the sacrament had at times
been distorted and misused. Better education of those hearing
confession was one result.

In 1614 the *Rituale Romanum* was published. While the ancient principle of "solemn penance" (the formal expulsion from

the Church on Ash Wednesday of those guilty of grave sins and their reconciliation on Holy Thursday) was retained, there is little evidence that solemn penance was widely used. The rite for private confession, also published in the *Rituale Romanum*, would remain in general use throughout the Catholic Church with only slight changes for four centuries, until changes were introduced following the Second Vatican Council.

The *Rituale Romanum* counseled the priest to begin with private prayer. The penitent, having carefully examined his conscience, was to kneel and make the sign of the cross, telling the priest how long it had been since the previous confession and whether any penance previously assigned had been completed. The penitent would then recite a short prayer of general confession and confess particular sins he or she had committed since the last confession. If necessary, the priest would ask about the frequency and circumstances, but was advised to be cautious and not ask unnecessary questions. Then, taking into account both the gravity of the sins and the condition and attitude of the penitent, he would offer counsel and impose a penance—for example almsgiving, fasting, and more frequent confession and communion—to assist the penitent's renewal and to remedy weakness.

Should the priest discover the penitent was lacking in basic religious understanding, he was required to provide the necessary instruction. Finally he granted absolution with these words: "May almighty God have mercy on you, forgive you your sins, and bring you to everlasting life." Then he raised his hand (a vestige of the early rite of the laying on of hands), extending it toward the penitent while making the sign of the cross and saying, "May the almighty and merciful Lord grant you pardon, absolution, and remission of your sins. May our Lord Jesus Christ absolve you from every bond of excommunication and interdict, insofar as I can and you need it. I absolve you from your sins, in the name of the Father, and of the Son, and of the Holy Spirit. Amen." (In later centuries the prayer of absolution was slightly shortened, though until the late twentieth century it was recited in Latin and was thus unintelligible to most people.)

The most recent development in the history of confession in the West is the new approach within the Catholic Church that grew out of the Second Vatican Council (1962–65). The Council's *Constitution on the Sacred Liturgy* had included a call for a reform of the rites and formulas of penance in order to better express the sacrament's nature and effect more clearly but provided no specific guidelines beyond bringing back the laying on of hands, the sacrament's visible sign during most of Christian history.

"According to Saint Cyprian," the document noted, "the imposition of hands was the sign of reconciliation and communion with the Church that is restored in penance—necessary because the living bond with the Church had been destroyed by sin. [The laying on of hands] signified reconciliation through the Holy Spirit." The Council placed renewed stress not only on private penitential practices, such as fasting, but also on sacrificial social action—almsgiving and service to others in need.

In 1973, eight years after the end of the Council, Pope Paul VI authorized publication of a new Order of Penance for the Catholic Church. Scripture readings were added to the revised rite and a more conversational style of confession was encouraged, as a consequence of which "reconciliation rooms"—in some cases glass-walled rooms that were part of the church building—were created in many parishes. Here priest and penitent could meet face-to-face, though with the option for the penitent to kneel behind a screen.

At least in many parts of western Europe in recent years, one can easily find Catholic parishes where there is no visible evidence of confession. Yet Fr. Michael Baxter, a professor of theology at Notre Dame University, tells me that the sacrament is "coming out of hibernation." He writes:

> *More and more students and also faculty members and people in administrative and maintenance jobs are discovering that self-help books that carefully avoid the word "sin" while trying to pump up self-esteem just don't get to the root of the problems in their lives—sins they have committed or patterns of sinful behavior that*

are destroying their lives. They are discovering there are corners that cannot be turned without repentance, confession and forgiveness.

"Confessions are still heard all day every day at St. Francis Church on 31st Street in New York City," my friend Tom Cornell, now a deacon, writes me, "and there is a line—not a long one, but a line. There is a small reconciliation room with a glass door. You can sit in a chair or kneel in a dark space separated from the priest by a grille. At least at St. Francis, most people seem to prefer the chair."

There are also communal confession services in many Catholic parishes. This is how a pastor not far from New York City describes such a service:

We begin with a hymn, then a greeting and opening prayer followed by a reading from the Old Testament, a psalm, a Gospel reading and homily. After this there is a guided examination of conscience followed by a prayer of sorrow for all the sins each person has committed. We pray the Our Father together and then there is the individual confession and the individual absolution of all those attending. This is done in the open in various parts of the church, mainly in the sanctuary. The private, individual confessions focus in on the most troublesome sins the penitent has committed. The private confessions are usually very brief. Then all recite together a general penance and prayer. There is finally a dismissal and closing hymn. It's a joyous event. I always sense a great deal of happiness and relief among those taking part.[21]

Perhaps one result of increasing contact between Christians of the East and the West is that the Orthodox custom of the penitent standing before an icon of Christ while the priest listens from the side will begin to find a wider acceptance. It would be a return to the practice of the early Church.

BASIC STORIES

Alluring Amsterdam, with its gleaming rings of canals circling the old town center, has a prosaic underside: it is a city built on sand and mud. Rising a hair's breadth above sea level, it was never the ideal location for urban construction even in an age of two-story buildings. Those famous steep-gabled brick houses built in the time of Rembrandt would have sunk long ago if it weren't for the pilings they stand on—tree trunks driven deep into the wet soil. Sadly, many an old Amsterdam house has been torn down because the pilings rotted away, while some of the survivors now lean at odd angles.

Basic stories are like the pilings that hold up the houses of Amsterdam. These are the stories at the foundation of our lives, reaching deep into the darkness and mystery beneath consciousness, shaping and arranging perceptions, revealing patterns and meaning.

Joseph Donders, a Dutch priest who has spent much of his life in Africa, once told me that he had learned from African culture that the most important person in any society is the storyteller. Nothing protects a person or a nation as much as a true story—or threatens it more than a false story. What worried him most about America, he said, was that its primary story is the cowboy movie —always a tale about how good men with guns save the community from evil men with guns. In film after film, killing rather than conversion is the solution. The classic scene is the gunfight on Main Street. This is the Gospel According to John Wayne.

In moments of crisis, it isn't ideologies or theories that guide us but our primary stories. True stories help make us capable of love and sacrifice and light up the path to the kingdom of God. False stories condemn us to nothingness and disconnection. Much depends on our story-foundation. If the stories we live by are false, our foundations rot and we sink into the mud.

My wife and I were talking about stories over lunch today. We recalled Steven Spielberg's film, *Indiana Jones and the Last Crusade*, a section of which is set in an imaginary catacomb beneath Venice, a port city of mud and canals much like Amsterdam. In one scene we find Jones inching his way through a skeleton-lined, rat-infested labyrinth toward a medieval tomb where, barely escaping death, he finds a stone coffin lid which provides an essential clue to locating the Holy Grail, the actual chalice used at the Last Supper, a cup that gives those who drink from it healing and eternal life. Spielberg is fascinated by principal religious relics. It was the Ark of the Covenant that Jones sought and found in his first movie.

Spielberg's stories often hurl us into a quest, if not for the sacred, then for the mysterious, magical, and legendary. The problem is that it all happens in a desacralized world. Such films confront us with a reality in which the sacred is never *here*, right where I'm standing, but somewhere over *there*. Indiana Jones never actually reaches the sacred even when his quest succeeds and he at last holds the elusive sacred object in his hands. He finds what he's looking for, but it doesn't find him. An archeologist whose vocation brings him on a daily basis to the border zone where science rubs against legend, myth, and mystery, he never manages to cross the border. Conversion never happens.

An Indiana Jones film gives us an infinitely resourceful hero and leaves us with a set of vivid images of a world in which special objects possessing magical powers have been hidden by our ancestors. Jones aspires to find and safeguard these sacred artifacts and to keep them, with their mythic powers, out of the hands of evil men. If he succeeds, a museum will be the better for it, and the world perhaps marginally safer.

This is the Gospel According to Indiana Jones. It's a story that entertains and excites but can't hold up a life.

The Bible is a collection of basic stories that have the potential, to the extent we make them our own, of helping us live, here and now, in the kingdom of God. But there is no way to enter or remain in that domain except through ongoing conversion, which in turn involves repentance, confession, and forgiveness. Were we to cut out of the Bible all the stories that have to do with repentance, confession, and forgiveness, the book would be reduced to a ghost of itself. The New Testament would disappear.

Consider several of the basic stories related in the four Gospels that in various ways throw light on repentance, confession, and forgiveness: the parable of the Prodigal Son; the man who was first forgiven, then healed of paralysis; the woman caught in adultery; the Pharisee and the tax collector; the woman who washed the feet of Christ with her tears; and the raising of Lazarus from the dead.

THE SON WHO RETURNS

The parable of the Prodigal Son forms the main part of the fifteenth chapter of Luke's Gospel. Few New Testament stories include so much detail. It's a parable not only about a particular father and son who lived two thousand years ago but about anyone urgently in need of forgiveness and love—a story about confession, pardon, and the healing of shattered relationships.

> *There was a man who had two sons; and the younger of them said to his father, "Father, give me the share of property that falls to me."*

Christ describes a young man so impatient to come into his inheritance and be independent that in effect he says to his father, "As far as I'm concerned, you're already dead. Give me now what would have come to me after your funeral. I want nothing more to do with you or with this house." We can only guess what prefaces the story. Perhaps the younger son saw his father as too strict or his home life too confining, too dull. Perhaps he felt less loved than his older brother who seemed always to be a model of good behavior.

Most of us need only to look in the mirror to catch a glimpse of younger brother: someone in a hurry to have what he wants and ready to neglect, even despise, those whom God intends him to love—parents, brothers and sisters, friends, neighbors, strangers, enemies. The young man of Christ's story is me.

And he divided his living between them.

With God-like generosity, the father agrees to do what his son asks, though he knows his son well enough to realize that all that the boy receives might as well be burned in the kitchen stove. The boy takes his inheritance and leaves, intending never to return. With money in his pocket, he is at last free of parents, free of his brother, free of domestic morals and good behavior, free of boredom, free to do as he pleases. He is unable to imagine how short-lived his adventure will be, how quickly the money will be spent, or to conceive that not a single person who enjoys the company of a reckless spender will want to see him once he is penniless, or in what loneliness and misery he will eventually find himself.

Not many days later, the younger son gathered all he had and took his journey into a far country, and there he squandered his property in loose living. And when he had spent everything, a great famine arose in that country, and he began to be in want. So he went and joined himself to one of the citizens of that country, who sent him into his fields to feed swine. He would gladly have fed on the pods that the swine ate; and no one gave him anything.

This was a story first told to Jews—thus there was a special poignancy in the detail about the boy being so cut off from his own people that he lived with pigs and ate their food. Jews regard swine as too filthy to raise or eat.

But when he came to himself he said, "How many of my father's hired servants have bread enough and to spare, but I perish here with hunger! I will arise and go to my father, and I will say to him, 'Father, I have sinned against heaven and before you; I am no longer worthy to be called your son; treat me as one of your hired servants.'" And he arose and came to his father.

Near starvation, he finally realizes what a hell he has made for himself. Every door is locked against him. People he had thought of as friends sneer at him. He has made himself filthy in body and soul. He knows he has renounced the claim to be anyone's son, yet in his desperation and misery dares hope his father might at least allow him to return home as a servant. Full of dismay for what he said to his father and what he did with his inheritance, he walks home in his rags, ready to confess his sins, to beg for work, and to ask for a corner to sleep in.

But while he was yet at a distance, his father saw him and had compassion, and ran and embraced him and kissed him.

The son cannot imagine the love his father has for him or the fact that, despite all the trouble he caused, he has been desperately missed. Far from being glad to be rid of the boy, the father has gazed day after day in prayer toward the horizon in hope of his son's return. Had he not been watching he would not have noticed his child in the distance and realized who it was. Instead of simply standing and waiting for him to reach the door, he ran to meet him, embracing his child, pouring out words of joy and welcome rather than reproof or condemnation.

And the son said to him, "Father, I have sinned against heaven and before you; I am no longer worthy to be called your son."

This is the son's confession compacted into a single sentence. It is the essence of any confession.

The moment of confession and reunion is what Rembrandt focused on in an etching he made in 1636. The father enfolds his son in much the way an Orthodox priest bends over a person who has completed his confession. The father's right arm gently rests on his son's back while his left hand supports his son's clasped hands. The arrangement of the father's feet suggests the act of having run toward his child. His face radiates compassion, forgiveness, and anguish for all his son has suffered. While the ravaged face of the kneeling son is marked with the hard times he has known, most of all we see his grief, remorse, and appeal for forgiveness. His hands are clasped in a gesture of urgent prayer. He cannot comprehend his father's joy.

But the father said to his servants, "Bring quickly the best robe, and put it on him; and put a ring on his hand, and shoes on his feet; and bring the fatted calf and kill it, and let us eat and make merry; for this my son was dead, and is alive again; he was lost, and is found." And they began to make merry.

In a stairway to the right two servants are bringing shoes and fresh clothing, though one of them turns his face aside, perhaps in aversion to the boy's smell. A maid, having pushed open a shuttered window, gazes with amazement at the miracle of reconciliation. Beneath her, Rembrandt has arranged father and son in the form of a triangle, a traditional symbol of the Holy Trinity. The restoration of mutual love between parent and child is an image of the restoration of communion for each repentant person with God. This moment of repentance, forgiveness, and reconciliation is also the theme of a huge painting by Rembrandt that now hangs in the Hermitage in St. Petersburg and is reproduced on this book's cover.

The story has another layer not hinted at in the etching: the resentment of an older brother.

Rembrandt etching of the "Return of the Prodigal Son"

*Now his elder son was in the field; and as he came and
drew near to the house, he heard music and dancing.
And he called one of the servants and asked what this
meant. And he said to him, "Your brother has come, and
your father has killed the fatted calf, because he has received him safe and sound." But he was angry and refused to go in. His father came out and entreated him,
but he answered his father, "Lo, these many years I have
served you, and I never disobeyed your command; yet
you never gave me a kid, that I might make merry with
my friends. But when this son of yours came, who has de-
voured your living with harlots, you killed for him the
fatted calf!" And he said to him, "Son, you are always
with me, and all that is mine is yours. It was fitting to
make merry and be glad, for this your brother was dead,
and is alive; he was lost, and is found."*

Hatred can burn hottest within a family. Siblings often bitterly resent each other. The first murder—the first war—involved
the sons of Adam and Eve: Cain and Abel. The older brother in
Christ's parable of the Prodigal Son, while no killer, represents
those who take pride in their obedience and good behavior but
who fall prey to self-righteousness. The "good boy" arrives home
from a day of labor to discover a celebration under way, his un-
missed brother at its center, and refuses to take part. Why such
joy and honor for someone whom he thought he had seen the last
of and whom he regards as worse than a thief? His father has to
reassure his older son that his love for him is as great as for his
younger son. "Your brother has risen from the grave," he explains. "Now you must rise with him." It was as hard for the older
brother to welcome the younger as it was for the younger to come
home in rags and failure.[1]

At a recent conference on confession in Oxford, Metropolitan
Anthony Bloom, a former physician who now heads the Russian
Orthodox Church in Britain, spoke about the Prodigal Son. "This
parable is the same experience we have in confession," he said.

"God longs for our return. He cries over our betrayals of him and of ourselves. At the moment we reappear, he rushes to greet us. We discover that we are longed for, we are awaited, we are loved even in our sinfulness, loved with a love that never diminishes, something other than the quiet and peaceful love the father has for the son who has never done wrong. We are met by a father who opens his arms, who is not a judge but a savior."

He noted too how much each of us resembles the son who took his inheritance and squandered it. "We are no different. All the time we take from God all that he would give, all that we want, and use it according to our own tastes. God gives us life. How do we use it? Occasionally we may think: 'Wasn't it kind of him to give me so many things that I want. It was God's—now it is mine.' Of course we don't dare to actually say it. We say it not directly but indirectly. It is a sin against God, a turning away that is more horrible than denying him. We cross the river from God's realm to Satan's, where life is more interesting. We leave God to cry over our betrayal. This is sin: turning our back on God for more interesting things. We turn our back on God—God who loved us into existence at risk to himself. We say to God, 'You are not interesting enough.' Still, we turn to him occasionally, for he is the provider. We demand more of our inheritance. We sin against God by discarding and despising his gifts. We sin against God in the way we treat people. Yet everyone is loved, loved to the measure of Christ's death on the cross. He descends into hell for us, to find us even there."[2]

THE MAN WHO WAS FORGIVEN, THEN HEALED

Mark's Gospel has no overture. From verse one we are off and running at breakneck speed with a bare minimum of detail to slow us down. After a terse account of John the Baptist, the baptism of Jesus, and the Bible's shortest report of the temptations Christ endured while in the desert, we hear about the launching of his ministry in Galilee—his call to repentance coupled with the proclamation that the kingdom of God is at hand. Next he calls the first disciples. All this happens in the first twenty verses of chapter one. With the next verse we arrive at the first of a series of healing miracles. In the twenty-five verses that follow, still in the first chapter, Christ heals a man possessed by an unclean spirit, restores the apostle Peter's mother-in-law, cures many ill with various diseases or suffering from demons, and cleanses a leper.

It is in chapter two that Mark slows down slightly, giving ten whole verses to another miracle, one more complex than any described in the first chapter.

And when he returned to Capernaum after some days, it was reported that he was at home.

Capernaum, a Roman administrative center and garrison town on the northwest shore of the Sea of Galilee, stood along a principal trading route. It became Jesus' second home. The ruins of the town's ancient synagogue were found by archeologists in 1905. Peter's home has also been tentatively identified nearby.

And many were gathered together, so that there was no longer room for them, not even about the door; and he was preaching the word to them.

Clearly Jesus' reputation as a preacher and healer was already established. People were streaming to his door to hear him teach, to ask him questions, and to seek his advice and help. Others came out of curiosity. Among those who came that day were four men carrying a relative or friend who was paralyzed.

And they came, bringing to him a paralytic carried by four men. And when they could not get near him because of the crowd, they removed the roof above him; and when

they had made an opening, they let down the pallet on
which the paralytic lay.

Perhaps the man they were caring for was in such a bad state
they simply couldn't wait for the crowd to dissipate or let them
through. In their desperation, they climbed onto the roof and broke
through, lowering the paralytic's stretcher through the hole. We
hear nothing in the story about Christ objecting to the damage they
caused—rather his admiration for the faith revealed in their action.

And when Jesus saw their faith, he said to the paralytic,
"My son, your sins are forgiven."

It seems he admires the faith of all five, not only the paralytic. The unnamed man—Jesus speaks to him as a "son"—had
been brought in the hope that Christ might cure him of paralysis,
but what he first received was liberation from a burden even
heavier than his dead limbs. Like the father who received back
his prodigal son, not simply accepting him in a limited way but
fully pardoning him, Jesus forgives an afflicted man who has not
even dared ask for what he is given.

Mark reveals no details about the man's past or what sins he
committed. One assumes they were grave. After many healing
miracles, apparently none involving forgiveness, in this instance
Christ's first concern was the man's heavily burdened conscience.
Body and soul are so intertwined that it can happen that a physical illness is linked to a spiritual condition and that the healing of
the soul is a precondition for recovery of the body. Apparently
Jesus recognized that without forgiveness, the man brought to
him would always remain paralyzed.

But what he did was problematic for some of those who were
present: "Who is this man to forgive? Does he even know what
he is forgiving? How can he? Does he think he's God?" Not
everyone present welcomed his words. No matter what healing
powers Jesus possesses, even prophets are not empowered to forgive sins.

Now some of the scribes were sitting there, questioning in their hearts, "Why does this man say this? It is blasphemy! Who can forgive sins but God alone?"

That any man would presume to forgive someone of all his sins was a scandal to the scribes who were present (scribe meaning a man whose scholarship regarding the law was such that he was esteemed as a rabbi and his views relied on by others). Their critical opinion at this moment had not been spoken aloud but would have been apparent in their faces and attitude.

And immediately Jesus, perceiving in his spirit what was in their thoughts, said to them, "Why do you harbor such questions in your hearts? Which is easier, to say to the paralytic, 'Your sins are forgiven,' or to say, 'Rise, take up your pallet and walk'? But that you may know that the Son of man has authority on earth to forgive sins"— he said to the paralytic—"I say to you, rise, take up your pallet and go home."

Healing the man's crippled body follows forgiveness of his sins, the physical healing being done not only for the sake of the paralytic but as a sign for others who doubt that Jesus has the right and power to forgive.

And he rose, and immediately took up the pallet and went out before them all; so that they were all amazed and glorified God, saying, "We never saw anything like this!"

Mark's close attention to this particular miracle connects with the declaration he made in his Gospel's first verse: that Jesus Christ is not simply a great teacher or a prophet but is the Son of God. Yet repeatedly the Son of God identifies himself as "Son of man." There are seventy examples cited in the Gospels, including one in the account of Christ healing the paralytic. What does the phrase mean?

Son of man—*bar nasa* in Hebrew—means a human being, a descendant of Adam and Eve. Yet men and women are empowered to forgive only sins committed against themselves, not others, still less sins against creation and against God. No one can offer all-encompassing forgiveness.

The only other biblical use of the phrase "son of man" is in the Books of Daniel and Enoch.[3] In these texts, "Son of Man" is the title used for a righteous one who stands before God, "the Ancient of Days." The Son of Man inaugurates the kingdom of God, reveals all hidden treasures, overcomes kings, is the staff of the righteous and holy, the light and hope of peoples, chosen before all ages, the Lord throughout eternity, by whom mankind is saved.

Christ's use of the term draws the reader of the Gospels, as it drew those who stood before him when the paralytic was healed, more deeply into the mystery of his own being: a human being who has powers associated with God. The miracle story Mark relates, revealing not only the Christ who heals but the Christ who forgives, forces the hearer to ponder the question Jesus put to Peter—"Who do you say I am?"—and brings us closer to Peter's confession, "You are the Christ, the Son of the living God." It is to Christ we turn in confession. The priest who is present is there only as Christ's witness. It is Christ who heals and forgives.

THE WOMAN CAUGHT IN ADULTERY

If you lived in Jerusalem or were there during periods when he was visiting the city, the much-talked-about Jesus would not be hard to find.

> *Early in the morning [Jesus, having spent the night outside the city on the Mount of Olives] came again to the temple; all the people came to him, and he sat down and taught them.* (Jn 8:2)

Each day he sat in the courtyard of the city's principal building, the Temple, listening and responding, telling stories and explaining their meaning. It was also here that he was tested with questions by which his enemies hoped to trap him. One such question was a matter of life and death for a certain woman.

> *The scribes and the Pharisees brought a woman who had been caught in adultery. Placing her in the midst they said to him, "Teacher, this woman has been caught in the very act of adultery. Now the law Moses commanded us to stone such. What do you say about her?" This they said to test him, that they might have some charge to bring against him.*

The Books of Leviticus and Deuteronomy prescribe execution as the punishment for men and women caught in the act of adultery (see Lev 20:10, Deut 22:22-24), though how often the sentence was carried out is unknown. In the event described by John, it is not clear why only the woman and not the man is threatened with stoning. Perhaps the man escaped; or perhaps he was untouchable because of his status and power.

In fact, the sin of the woman and her fate were of secondary interest to those who brought her before Jesus. They confronted him with her, confident that he would be the loser no matter what answer he gave. If he said her life should be spared, he was openly rejecting the law of Moses and thus the foundation of Jewish life. Probably this is what they expected, since they were aware of his stress on mercy. Should he dare denounce an ordinance that sanctioned stoning, they would have solid grounds, from his own mouth, for bringing charges against him. On the other hand, if he blessed her execution, clearly he was not the man of mercy and guardian of life he was reputed to be. Those drawn to him would be disillusioned and perhaps disaffected. For those who opposed him, the question seemed a perfect way to trap him. The woman's sin was only a weapon to be used to condemn not her but him.

Jesus bent down and wrote with his finger on the ground.

What did he write? There is nothing in the Gospel to help us answer the question, though the author regards the action as worth mentioning. Perhaps Jesus wrote passages from the Law and the Prophets. (From Matthew's Gospel we know that Jesus sometimes recited a verse from Hosea: "I desire mercy and not sacrifice" [Hos 6:6; Mt 9:13, 12:7].) Or perhaps he listed some of the sins that are often committed but seldom punished by one's neighbors: lying, stealing, cheating, deception, acts of violence, undetected adultery, idolatry. Nearly all who have grown into adulthood can recall many sins for which they have never been made to pay any penalty but which cause their memories to burn with shame. Or perhaps Jesus wrote down the names of some of those present who had committed grave sins which they hoped were unknown. The prophet Jeremiah had said, "Those who turn away from You shall be written in the earth, for they have forsaken the LORD, the fountain of living water" (Jer 17:13).

And as they continued to ask him, he stood up and said to them, "Let him who is without sin among you be the first to throw a stone at her."

It was a brilliant answer, one that not only saved the woman's life but has saved countless lives ever since. It wasn't seditious. Jesus didn't attack the law or call for its overthrow. He didn't justify or minimize the woman's sin. He didn't accuse or shame anyone. He didn't even preach mercy and forgiveness. He simply suggested that the first stone be thrown by a sinless person. The woman's accusers found themselves accused, not by the words of Jesus but by their own consciences. Which of us is not a sinner? And if such a spotless person were present, would he or she wish to take part in the killing of another?

And once more he bent down and wrote with his finger on the ground. But when they heard it, they went away,

*one by one, beginning with the eldest, and Jesus was left
alone with the woman standing before him.*

Again a deep silence. Again unspoken words drawn on the
ground. Jesus wasn't even looking at the faces around him. In
the silence the accusers withdrew, eldest first—they who carried
the heaviest burden of sin. Finally not one accuser remained,
only the woman.

*Jesus looked up and said to her, "Woman, where are
they? Has no one condemned you?" She said, "No one,
Lord." And Jesus said, "Neither do I condemn you; go,
and do not sin again."*

It's a brief exchange. The one sinless person, himself, speaks
a few words that give her back her life. Even then he refrains
from any word of censure, instead making a single request—that
she sin no more.

In fact throughout the Gospel, no matter how great the sin or
provocation, no one is killed or injured by Jesus or his followers.
The one injury caused by a disciple—Peter wounding a man who
had come to arrest Jesus in the Garden of Gethsemane—provided the occasion for Christ's last healing miracle before his
crucifixion.

What is my part in this drama? Am I the woman caught in
adultery, even if no one else knows the sins that haunt me? Is my
conscience like the earth on which Christ silently is writing words
which only I can read? Or am I one of those in the crowd, poised
to hurl deadly stones at the guilty? Is it to me that he says, "Let he
who is without sin cast the first stone"? Or am I both the one
judged and the one judging?

Confession provides a short cut. Rather than waiting for others to drag me to a place of judgment and punishment, or hoping
that those with stones in their hands and stone-like hearts will be
moved to mercy by recalling Christ's words, I admit my guilt and
beg for forgiveness.

THE PHARISEE AND THE TAX COLLECTOR

In the Orthodox calendar, you know Lent is just around the corner when it's the Sunday of the Pharisee and the Tax Collector. A week later it will be the Sunday of the Prodigal Son, then Last Judgment Sunday, then Forgiveness Sunday, with the Great Fast starting the next day: four Sundays of wading into Lent. The reading of the Gospel story of the Pharisee and the tax collector (Lk 18:9-14) is always a border-crossing moment.

*He also told this parable to some who trusted in them-
selves that they were righteous and despised others.*

Even before Luke tells the story there is summing up of its main issue: the danger of being conscientious in one's religious life while looking down on others who seem to ignore God and live disreputable lives.

*Two men went up into the temple to pray, one a Pharisee
and the other a tax collector.*

For the Pharisees, the Law of Moses wasn't just a subject to study but a text guiding life through every hour of each day. It was Jewish disobedience to the Law, the Pharisees believed, which had brought about the severe punishment of the Babylonian exile. Pharisees prayed often, were active in the synagogue, maintained Jewish tradition, kept the fasts, tithed their possessions, were faithful to their spouses, made donations to the poor, and tended to be among the most exemplary members of society. Many were artisans. While there were Pharisees like Joseph of Arimethia who became disciples of Jesus, many others were disturbed by his approach to the Law, which some saw as allowing disobedience to the implications of God's commandments.

It isn't that Jesus took the Law of Moses lightly. Though occasionally accused of being a law breaker, he only opposed making men slaves of a rigid interpretation of the law, so that it was law men worshiped rather than God. "The sabbath was made for man, not man for the sabbath," he said (Mk 2:27). Acts of mercy and healing, he insisted by word and example, were not a form of labor.

One of the big differences between Pharisees and tax collectors was that the Pharisees were not Rome's partners. Tax collectors, on the other hand, were among Rome's principal collaborators, men well rewarded for their repulsive work, retaining a percentage of the money they collected and thus made members of the tiny class of wealthy people. They were regarded by their fellow Jews as extortionists who worshiped money rather than God. *Butler's Lives of the Saints* notes that "Jews abhorred tax collectors to the extent they refused to marry into a family which had a tax collector among its members, banished them from communion in religious worship, and shunned them in all affairs of civil society and commerce."[4] One of the scandals of the New Testament is that one of Jesus' primary disciples, Matthew, author of the first Gospel, had been a tax collector before he was made an apostle.

The Pharisee stood and prayed thus with himself, "God, I thank you that I am not like other men, extortioners, unjust, adulterers, or even like this tax collector. I fast twice a week, I give tithes of all that I get."

The Pharisee described is an honorable, God-fearing man, if complacent and self-absorbed. If he were only thanking God for giving him the strength to keep the Law of Moses, Christ might praise him, but instead Christ condemns him for regarding a neighbor with contempt while admiring himself. We see in the Pharisee's heart an absence of love.

If we had been in the synagogue ourselves and had noticed the tax collector, we might later have described him as a nervous rich man who seemed to be upset about something. Christ allows us to look into the man's heart. Here we discover someone deeply ashamed of what he has been doing, far more critical of himself

than any Pharisee. He has been moved to enter the synagogue but
dares not approach the front or even to raise his eyes toward the
alcove where the sacred texts are kept.

> *But the tax collector, standing far off, would not even lift*
> *up his eyes to heaven, but beat his breast, saying, "God,*
> *be merciful to me a sinner!"*

This is among the shortest, simplest prayers in the Bible. In
the early Church it evolved into the Jesus Prayer, or the Prayer of
the Heart, as it is sometimes called:

> *Lord Jesus Christ, Son of God, be merciful to me, a sinner!*

Many millions of people use this one sentence prayer, or
variations of it, again and again each day. In whatever form it is
used, it is an urgent cry of the heart for God's mercy and forgiveness. The prayer encourages an attitude in radical opposition to
self-righteousness. God will not be merciful to me because I am
able to point at someone else who—at least as it seems to me—is
doing even worse.

Jesus is not urging us to become tax collectors nor does he
mock the virtues of the Pharisee. What he warns us against is dar-
ing to think of ourselves as "better than" or "dearer to God than"
anyone else.

Consider the person approaching the chalice while reciting
the traditional Orthodox communion prayer, "I believe O Lord
and I confess that you are truly the Son of God, who came into
the world to save sinners, of whom I am first." Not "first" except
for Stalin or Hitler or whomever I most love to hate, but myself
as the worst of sinners. This is not because I imagine historians
will feel obliged to take note of my sins, but because I cannot
imagine anyone doing a worse job of hearing and responding to
Christ's voice than myself, a person who has had so many more
blessings than history's most famous sinners.

The repentant tax collector, who may later have become the apostle Matthew, gives an example of poverty of heart.

I tell you, this man went down to his house justified rather than the other; for every one who exalts himself will be humbled, but he who humbles himself will be exalted.

THE WOMAN WHO WASHED THE FEET OF CHRIST WITH HER TEARS

Another story, in Luke 7, contrasts a Pharisee named Simon with a repentant woman who may have been a prostitute. In Christian tradition she has often been regarded as Mary Magdalene, a woman freed of seven demons, who is mentioned later in chapter eight of Luke's Gospel.

One of the Pharisees asked him to eat with him, and he went into the Pharisee's house, and sat at table.

Was Jesus a prophet? Could he even be the promised Messiah for whom Israel was waiting? These were questions many were asking, including Simon. Perhaps he hoped that talking with him over a meal would help him decide. But he found he had not only Jesus as a guest, and with him some of his disciples, but also a notorious woman whom he would never have asked into his home.

And behold, a woman of the city, who was a sinner, when she learned that he was sitting at table in the Pharisee's house, brought an alabaster flask of ointment, and standing behind him at his feet, weeping, she began to wet his feet with her tears, and wiped them with the hair of her head, and kissed his feet, and anointed them with the ointment.

Apparently the woman had been among those who had been listening to Jesus earlier and was so affected by his words and manner that she followed him into Simon's house. She had with her an alabaster flask of perfumed ointment which she may have intended to use to oil his hair but was so overcome with remorse for the state of her life and gratitude for his teaching that instead she wept on his feet, washing them with her tears, drying them with her hair, then anointing them with ointment and kissing them: a flood-like outpouring of love.

> *Now when the Pharisee who had invited him saw it, he said to himself, "If this man were a prophet, he would have known who and what sort of woman this is who is touching him, for she is a sinner."*

The fact that Jesus allows her to touch him and says no word of reprimand for who she is and what she has done convinces the Pharisee that Jesus is no prophet. The Hebrew word is *nabi*—someone called by God. A prophet is someone able to see things as God sees them and to rebuke sinners on God's behalf. Here was a woman who had scandalized decent people. If Jesus were truly a man of God, surely he would denounce her sin and send her away. Instead he has let her tend to him as if she were his hostess.

Jesus understands what Simon is thinking and responds by telling him a parable.

> *And Jesus answering said to him, "Simon, I have something to say to you." And he answered, "What is it, Teacher?" "A certain creditor had two debtors; one owed five hundred denarii, and the other fifty. When they could not pay, he forgave them both. Now which of them will love him more?" Simon answered, "The one, I suppose, to whom he forgave more." And he said to him, "You have judged rightly."*

A denarius was a small Roman coin made of silver. At the time it would have been a day's pay for a laborer. The Good Samaritan gave two denarii to the inn keeper. In Revelation, it is mentioned that a ration of wheat cost a denarius in time of famine. Five hundred denarii was a fortune.

Having told the parable, for the first time Jesus turned toward the crying woman who had so offended his host.

> *"Do you see this woman? I entered your house, you gave me no water for my feet, but she has wet my feet with her tears and wiped them with her hair. You gave me no kiss, but from the time I came in she has not ceased to kiss my feet. You did not anoint my head with oil, but she has anointed my feet with ointment."*

Washing a guest's feet, oiling his hair, giving him a kiss of greeting—these were ordinary Semitic gestures of hospitality which it seems Simon had neglected to offer Jesus, perhaps because he was so unsure what to make of him. It was the uninvited guest who did what the host had failed to do, and more.

In the parable of forgiven debtors, it was the person who owed the larger sum who was most grateful for the erasing of an obligation—but in the woman's case it was not a debt of money that was at issue but a debt to heaven for having so misused her life. Now Jesus makes it clear to Simon that indeed he knows who it is who has washed his feet and what painful memories burden her.

> *"Therefore I tell you, her sins, which are many, are forgiven, for she loved much; but he who is forgiven little, loves little."*

Then finally he speaks to her, saying:

> *"Your sins are forgiven."*

In this case the confession was not even a confession of words but of tears and kisses.

Then those who were at table with him began to say among themselves, "Who is this, who even forgives sins?"

Again the question: Who is this man? Who but God can forgive?

And he said to the woman, "Your faith has saved you; go in peace."

This is similar to the end of any confession: an assurance that you are saved—you are already in the kingdom of God—and the instruction to live a life of peace with God and neighbor. It is like saying: Your life has a new beginning.

THE RAISING OF LAZARUS

Three times in the Gospels we are told stories of Jesus bringing the dead back to life: a child raised from her death bed who immediately afterward asks for something to eat (she wanted spaghetti, our daughter Anne was convinced); a young man whose body was being carried to its place of burial; and finally Lazarus, not only dead but dead and buried.

Now a certain man was ill, Lazarus of Bethany, the village of Mary and her sister Martha. It was Mary who anointed the Lord with ointment and wiped his feet with her hair, whose brother Lazarus was ill. So the sisters sent to him, saying, "Lord, he whom you love is ill." But when Jesus heard it he said, "This illness is not unto death; it is for the glory of God, so that the Son of God may be glorified by means of it."

Bethany is a village on the east side of the Mount of Olives within easy walking distance of Jerusalem. It was in Bethany just six days before Passover and the rush of events that would follow that Mary poured a costly perfume on Christ's feet and dried his feet with her hair, scandalizing Judas and prompting Jesus to say that she was preparing his body for burial—not words his disciples wanted to hear (Jn 12:1-8).

We are given a glimpse of the characters of these remarkable sisters in a story Luke tells about Jesus' first visit to their home. While Martha busied herself preparing a meal, Mary sat at the feet of Jesus questioning him. Her absence from the kitchen so annoyed Martha that finally she directed an appeal to their guest: "Lord, do you not care that my sister has left me to serve alone? Tell her then to help me." Christ replied, "Martha, Martha, you are anxious and troubled about many things; one thing is needful. Mary has chosen the better part, which shall not be taken away from her."

In the kitchen, smoke is rising more from Martha than from the stove. If we had only this story to draw from, we might be tempted to assume that Mary is the real disciple, while Martha the sort of person too busy with life's details to notice those things that reveal life's meaning. But we see the two sisters from another angle after Lazarus's death.

It had been a relief to his disciples that Jesus, despite news of Lazarus's illness, delayed going to Bethany. They knew Jesus would himself be in mortal danger if he were anywhere near Jerusalem. Yet finally, with Passover fast approaching, he set out on the long walk from Galilee to Jerusalem intending to stop in Bethany on the way—his final great journey before his crucifixion. Some of the disciples were hesitant to accompany him—their lives too would be in danger. It was Thomas, soon to earn the nickname "Doubting Thomas," who said, "Let us also go, that we may die with him."

By the time they arrived in Bethany, it was too late:

Now when Jesus came, he found that Lazarus had already been in the tomb four days.

Vermeer's "Christ in the House of Mary and Martha" c.1655

It was a tomb similar to the one that would be used a few days later for the body of Jesus—a vault carved into a hillside and sealed with a large circular stone that rolled along a groove. Inside lay the corpse of Lazarus, bound in linen cloth.

Bethany was near Jerusalem, about two miles off, and many of the Jews had come to Martha and Mary to console them concerning their brother.

Lazarus and his sisters were respected and loved by many, not only by neighbors in Bethany but also by friends in Jerusalem. They had come for the burial several days before and either stayed on in Bethany or returned each day to console both the mourning sisters and each other. It was a culture in which such events as marriage and burial were spread over days rather than hours.

When Martha heard that Jesus was coming, she went and met him, while Mary sat in the house. Martha said to Jesus, "Lord, if you had been here, my brother would not have died. And even now I know that whatever you ask from God, God will give you."

There is no welcome this time from the sister who had once chosen "the better part." Far from wishing to sit at his feet, Mary doesn't want to see him. It is Martha of the kitchen who responds to the news that Christ is approaching, meeting him at the edge of the village. Both sisters are deeply disappointed by his late arrival—Jesus has failed to meet their expectations. Martha puts their complaint plainly, as if to say, "If you hadn't dragged your feet, my brother would be alive." It's an accusation. Yet she also declares her belief that whatever he prays for will happen. Then begins a dialogue:

Jesus said to her, "Your brother will rise again." Martha said to him, "I know that he will rise again in the resurrection at the last day."

There was a long-running argument among Jews about what happened after death. Some, like Martha, anticipated a general resurrection and final judgment at the end of history. Others dismissed such beliefs as wishful thinking. Apart from a few brief accounts of the dead being restored to life—but not eternal life—by Elijah and Elisha (1 Kings 17:17-24; 2 Kings 4:18-37), the Old Testament is silent about resurrection. The Jewish historian Josephus as well as the New Testament report that the Pharisees believed in the resurrection of the dead while the Sadducees and Samaritans did not (see, for example, Mt 22:23 and Acts 23:8).

At key moments in the New Testament, Jesus makes "I am" declarations about himself: "I am the door, I am the light, I am the way." Now, facing a woman whose brother has died, comes one of the most important "I am" statements:

Jesus said to her, "I am the resurrection and the life; he who believes in me, though he die, yet shall he live, and whoever lives and believes in me shall never die."

Resurrection is no longer simply a hope, belief, concept, or theory. Resurrection exists in the person of Jesus. Resurrection—eternal life free of disease and sorrow—is a dimension of existence in God, the source of life, in whom there is no death. While acknowledging that death exists—Lazarus has died and been buried, as everyone present knows—Jesus tells Martha that whoever believes in him will not only live but become an immortal.

Then he asks Martha:

"Do you believe this?"

She responds with more than an affirmation:

"Yes, Lord; I believe that you are the Christ, the Son of God, he who is coming into the world."

These are words similar to Peter's declaration of faith that Jesus is "the Christ, the Son of the Living God." These are moments of absolute recognition.

It is only at this point that Martha decides to pry her sister out of the house and bring her to Jesus, referring to him as the teacher.

When she had said this, she went and called her sister Mary, saying quietly, "The Teacher is here and is calling for you." And when Mary heard it, she rose quickly and went to him.

Perhaps it was a note of excited expectation in her sister's voice that made Mary let go of her estrangement and come with haste to the place where Jesus and his disciples were standing.

Now Jesus had not yet come to the village, but was still in the place where Martha had met him. When the Jews who were with her in the house, consoling her, saw Mary rise quickly and go out, they followed her, supposing that she was going to the tomb to weep there.

This is the first time that weeping has been specifically mentioned, yet we can assume this had been the main activity of most of the people present since Lazarus died.

Then Mary, when she came where Jesus was and saw him, fell at his feet, saying to him, "Lord, if you had been here, my brother would not have died."

In the foreground of icons of the raising of Lazarus, we see both Martha and Mary prostrating themselves at Christ's feet. Prostration is one of the physical postures both of worship and appeal. Mary had once been at Christ's feet—now they both are. Mary echoes Martha's protest that Jesus had come too slowly to

Bethany. All the while both sisters are crying, as are all those mourners who followed Mary from the house.

> *When Jesus saw her weeping, and the Jews who came with her also weeping, he was deeply moved in spirit and troubled; and he said, "Where have you laid him?" They said to him, "Lord, come and see."*

Now comes one of the shortest sentences in the Bible:

Jesus wept.

This is the second time in the Gospel that these same two words are used. On another occasion, we know from Luke, Christ wept while looking at Jerusalem from a distance, foreseeing the city's destruction by Rome's army and the immense suffering that Jews would endure in those calamitous days and in the exile to follow. Here at Bethany his weeping is joined with the sorrow of a community of friends who feel their hearts torn open by Lazarus's terrible absence from their lives. "Christ wept," Saint Augustine comments, "that we might learn to weep."

> *So the Jews said, "See how he loved him!" But some of them said, "Could not he who opened the eyes of the blind man have kept this man from dying?"*

Everyone present is moved by Christ's grief. They see he is not a person who keeps an imperial distance from the feelings and pain of others, not a man holding himself aloof from ordinary human emotions. At the same time, they are aware of at least some of his healing miracles. In particular they recall Jesus giving sight to the man born blind who used to beg not far from the gate that people from Jerusalem would pass through when walking to Bethany, a story John tells in the ninth chapter of his Gospel. Like the sisters, they wonder why he failed to prevent his friend's death.

Then Jesus, deeply moved again, came to the tomb; it was a cave, and a stone lay upon it.

"Deeply moved" suggests he was still weeping and that he was speaking through his tears.

Jesus said, "Take away the stone."

What he asked for was as distasteful as it would be for anyone today to unearth a coffin and expose the decomposing body within. It is practical Martha who voices the objection everyone present must have been thinking:

"Lord, by this time there will be a stench, for he has been dead four days."

Jesus reminds her of the conversation they had had only minutes before, when she had told him that she believed in the resurrection and he had responded by saying "I am the resurrection."

"Did I not tell you that if you would believe you would see the glory of God?"

Christ often links healing to belief—what seems impossible can happen if not blocked by disbelief.

Several men do as Christ asks, though probably with some reluctance. In the traditional icon of Lazarus's resurrection, we see the stone rolled away while those standing near the tomb's entrance hold their robes against their noses to muffle the reek of death. Christ prays before the open grave.

So they took away the stone. And Jesus lifted up his eyes and said, "Father, I thank you that you have heard me. I knew that you hear me always, but I have said this on account of the people standing by, that they may believe that you sent me."

What might have been a silent prayer is said aloud. Through it we understand that bringing Lazarus back to life is done not only to relieve two sisters and their friends but to help them—and all who hear this story—understand who he is and by whom he has come into our world.

When he had said this, he cried with a loud voice, "Lazarus, come out." The dead man came out, his hands and feet bound with bandages, and his face wrapped with a cloth. Jesus said to them, "Unbind him, and let him go."

Lazarus has been brought back to life though this is not yet eternal life—another death awaits him. Death has become a memory as well as an expectation. A man who had breathed his last, who had been buried and begun to rot in his grave, finds himself seeing and breathing again and once again must find his place in the world, the same man and yet changed. Perhaps returning to life is a harder struggle than letting go of life. If you've seen the film *Cast Away,* with Tom Hanks playing a Lazarus-like role, you can imagine how difficult the return to "normal life" must be for death's survivors. Nothing is as it was or ever can be again. Death is no longer the enemy it was.

Not many years ago Nancy and I venerated the skull of Lazarus in the cathedral at Autun, among France's most beautiful Romanesque churches, an ancient center of pilgrimage. The tradition is that later in life Lazarus joined his sisters in missionary activity that finally brought them among the Celts and Romans in Gaul, today's France. Pious legend or actual history? Did they really travel so far from Bethany? We'll find out in heaven. For the moment we can only be certain that from the early days of Christianity, there has been a special bond connecting the French with Lazarus, Mary, and Martha. While the legend contains whimsical details—a small boat without sail gliding across the Mediterranean bearing three passengers—the core of the story is not impossible. Given what had happened in this family, it is hard to be-

Icon of the raising of Lazarus

lieve they could be anything but missionaries, finding it unthinkable to return to life as it was before Christ's voice brought Lazarus in his grave clothes back among the living. When he was raised from the dead, not only Lazarus but all three were unbound and released.

"The Lord's acts are not only deeds, but signs," Augustine says in his commentary on the Gospel of John (Tractate 49). Seen as a sign, Lazarus's resurrection has enduring meaning in the present. It is evidence of Christ's readiness, through forgiveness, to restore to life anyone who has become corpse-like because of sin.

For Augustine, Lazarus is not only a particular man who once lived and died and lived again in Bethany. He serves as a symbol of the "death" that penetrates anyone's life. Augustine interprets the four days Lazarus was in the tomb symbolically: the first day represents our inheritance of death from Adam and Eve; the second day the death that comes to us for violating conscience, "the law written in the heart"; the third day the death for violating the Law given to Moses; the fourth day, the death that comes through abandoning the Gospel. This deepest death, Augustine writes, belongs to whoever has first embraced the Gospel and then despised it, who has been baptized but returns to his old ways. It's the death of the "fourth day," says Augustine bluntly, that makes a man stink like a four-day-old cadaver.

None of the "deaths" Augustine is concerned with are the kind that require undertakers and coffins. They are rather death disguised as life: having eyes but not seeing, having ears but not hearing, having a heart but not loving, having a mind but lacking faith, being exposed to miracles and yawning. It is the death of gradually becoming mired in my worst habits, being increasingly untroubled by my own selfishness and more and more disconnected from others—the death of making myself at home in hell even while still living in this world.

The tomb and the linen-wrapped body within it can be viewed metaphorically.

The stone sealing the place of burial is all that we heap upon ourselves that drags us toward hell rather than heaven. The stone is our idolatries—not stone carvings but ideologies, slogans, tribal prides that sanction hatred, private goals which become all important, rules that become ends in themselves.

The grave is the darkness we gather around ourselves by no longer searching for God's image in others. It is a self-absorption that turns others into objects to be used, or ignored if no use is found. It is having no sense of God's presence.

The grave clothing binding the corpse is our numbed paralysis: the inability to reach out, to help, to love.

Yet there is a way out of the tomb. Confession is my admitting out loud the extent of my self-made death, the many ways in which I have distanced myself from Christ and denied him, in action and thought if not in word. "When you despise Christ," says Augustine in his commentary on the raising of Lazarus, "you lie in the arms of death...but when you confess, you come forth."

STANDING AT THE FOUR CROSSROADS

No writer has explored more carefully than Dostoevsky the way a sin is justified in the doer's mind before it is committed, the innate human urge to confess afterward, the struggle not to confess, and the healing made possible by confession—all lessons Dostoevsky learned in the crucible of life. A writer whose later work always had a religious core, he came to faith the hard way.

In 1849, the twenty-eight-year-old Dostoevsky had been sentenced to death for his radical associations and activities in St. Petersburg. He was standing at the place of execution, in view of the firing squad, when his death sentence was commuted by the tsar. Days later, the hair shaven off one side of his head and wearing a convict's black-and-white-striped uniform, he was sent in chains to Siberia. While he was on his way the wife of another convict managed to give him a copy of the New Testament along with a ten-ruble note hidden in the cover. He kept the book with him for the rest of his life.

He spent the first four years "packed like a sardine" inside a vermin-infested prison barrack, a rotting building that was stuffy in summer and freezing in winter, a world without any privacy or safety. He wasn't permitted to write a single letter. Yet there was a certain blessing in his sojourn in the "lower depths," a term often used by radical Russian intellectuals who contemplated the ordinary people—the *narod*—from a safe distance. Tolstoy might oc-

"Portrait of Dostoevsky" by Fritz Eichenberg,
from The Grand Inquisitor

casionally labor with his peasants and wear similar clothing, but
at night he slept on silk sheets. Dostoevsky lived and slept day
and night for years among some of Russia's poorest. Among the
"unfortunate ones," as Russians often called those in prison, he
rethought the foundations of his life.

A religious awakening occurred. He began to consider that the
Gospel might be true and that the Church—the guardian of the
Gospel—might be something more than a social institution whose
main task was blessing the tsar and the activities of the state.

Finally allowed to engage in correspondence in 1854, he related to a friend how he had come to thirst for faith "as withered
grass thirsts for water":

> *I'm a child of the age, a child of doubt and unbelief, and
> even, I'm certain, till the day they close the lid of my cof-
> fin. What terrible torment this thirst to believe has cost
> me and is still costing me, the stronger it becomes in my
> soul, the stronger are the arguments against it. And de-
> spite all this God sends me moments of great tranquility,
> moments during which I love and find I am loved by oth-
> ers. It was during such a moment that I formed within
> myself a symbol of faith[1] in which all is clear and sacred
> for me. The symbol [creed] is very simple, and here is
> what it is: to believe that there is nothing more beautiful,
> more profound, more sympathetic, more reasonable,
> more courageous, and more perfect than Christ; and
> there not only isn't, but I tell myself with a jealous love,
> there cannot be. More than that—if someone succeeded
> in proving to me that Christ was outside the truth, and if,
> indeed, the truth was outside Christ, I would sooner re-
> main with Christ than with the truth.[2]*

It is in Dostoevsky's Siberian years that the novels of his later life
have their roots.

In *Crime and Punishment*, Dostoevsky's central figure is
Raskolnikov, a sullen student living in a shabby rented room in St.

Petersburg. He regards himself as modern, belonging to a new age in which God and compassion have been banished by science. Penniless, he is obsessed with loathing for a moneylender to whom he is in debt and slowly becomes a murderer in his imagination. It occurs to him that murder is not always regarded as a crime—those who commit crime on a huge scale, people like Napoleon, are regarded as national heroes, benefactors of humanity and giants of history despite the desolation and carnage they instigate. Such supermen, refusing to be shackled by mere morality, "make a new law by transgressing an old one." Raskolnikov decides that by killing the moneylender, a selfish old woman whom no one will mourn, he would be saving many families "from destitution, from decay, from ruin, from depravity" while at the same time relieving his own poverty. He imagines that afterwards, liberated from destitution with the money he has obtained from the chest in her bedroom, he will be free to "devote himself to the service of humanity and the common good." In such a case, he reasons, murder, far from being a sin, would be just and good. "One death for hundreds of lives—it's simple arithmetic!"

Yet when he commits his carefully planned and philosophically justified murder, things do not go entirely as intended. He kills the moneylender but discovers that a simple-minded young woman, Lizaveta, has witnessed his deed and so murders her as well so that she cannot testify against him. The hatchet Raskolnikov had hidden in his jacket is now reddened not only with a miser's blood but also with that of a saintly innocent who never harmed or hated anyone.[3]

He has been clever in committing his crime. No trail of clues connects him to the two dead women. Even so an intuitive policeman, Porfiry Petrovich, finds more and more reasons to regard Raskolnikov as the guilty one. Petrovich sees Raskolnikov's nearly dead soul—his heart "chafed by theories"—and understands that this young man's only hope is confession and repentance. He plays a part in rescuing Raskolnikov from the hell into which he has locked himself. Porfiry Petrovich is able to say to Raskolnikov that "God is waiting for you" and to tell him that the suffering he will have to endure as a prisoner can be, after all, a good thing. He points out to Raskolnikov that his crime, terrible as it was, might have been worse: "If you'd come up with a different theory, you might have done something a hundred million times more hideous!" He delays arresting Raskolnikov in the hope that he will "become like a sun" and confess.

But Raskolnikov's principal rescuer is Sonya, a young woman of deep Christian faith who has become a prostitute for the sake of her impoverished family's survival. When at last Raskolnikov admits to her his terrible secret, it is Sonya who tells him that his only hope is confession—confession to God, to the police, to a priest, to everyone.

> *"What to do?" she exclaimed, suddenly jumping up from her place, and her eyes, still full of tears, suddenly flashed. "Stand up!" (She seized him by the shoulder; he rose, looking at her almost in amazement.) "Go now, this minute, stand in the crossroads, bow down, and first kiss the earth you've defiled, then bow to the whole world, on all four sides, and say aloud to everyone: 'I have killed!' Then God will send you life again. Will you go? Will you?"*

Sonya has a copy of the New Testament from which she used to read aloud to Lizaveta. Raskolnikov asks her to read to him from the same book. She turns to the eleventh chapter of John's Gospel but at first has difficulty making any sound, she is so overcome with emotion. Finally she starts reading: "Now a certain man was sick, named Lazarus, of Bethany...." It is the story of Jesus' friend who died and four days later, from within his tomb, was called back to life. Jesus asks Martha if she believes in the resurrection of the dead. She says she believes her brother will be raised back to life at the end of time. Jesus responds, "I am the resurrection and the life." Sonya by now is reading with strength in her voice, as if she herself were Martha: "Yes, Lord, I believe that you are the Christ, the Son of God...."

Sonya assures Raskolnikov that his only hope is to confess, accept suffering, and thus redeem himself. Otherwise, though outwardly free and part of normal society, his unspeakable secret will cut him off from everyone around him, even his mother and sister.

Raskolnikov realizes that in confessing the truth to Sonya, a door has opened at least a crack. They sit

> *side by side, sad and crushed, as if they had been washed up alone on a deserted shore after a storm. He looked at Sonya and felt how much of her love was on him, and, strangely, suddenly felt it heavy and painful to be loved like that. Yes, it was a strange and terrible feeling!*

She offers Raskolnikov a small cross that had belonged to the murdered Lizaveta and promises him to share in his suffering and to help him bear his cross. Lizaveta's cross is a gift he cannot yet accept, nor is he yet capable of surrendering to Sonya's counsel. In the days that follow he considers escaping to America. At other moments he contemplates suicide. But finally he goes to the police station and confesses the double murder.

The punishment for murder in late-nineteenth-century Russia was not execution but imprisonment and hard labor in Siberia. Raskolnikov gets a relatively short sentence—eight years, the length of Dostoevsky's own period of imprisonment and exile. The judge explains that it would have been a longer sentence, but he has taken note of the fact that Raskolnikov made no effort during his trial to excuse himself on the basis of illness or temporary insanity nor ever used any of the stolen money for his own benefit. There was also the fact that several persons testified on his behalf about ways he had helped them.

Sonya eventually follows him to Siberia, living not far from the prison and doing all she can to help not only Raskolnikov but also other "unfortunate ones."

It is while in prison, a year after his conviction, that the full horror of his two murders dawns on Raskolnikov. Real repentance begins and with it floods of tears.

In the last paragraph of *Crime and Punishment*, Raskolnikov holds in his hands the New Testament, a book he has been keeping under his pillow but not yet opened.

> *He took the book out mechanically. It belonged to her, it was the same one from which she had read to him about the raising of Lazarus. At the beginning of his hard labor he had thought she would hound him with religion, would be forever talking about the Gospels and forcing books on him. But to his greatest amazement, she never once spoke of it, never once even offered him the Gospels. He had asked her for it himself... and she had silently brought him the book. He had not even opened it yet.*
>
> > *Nor did he open it now, but a thought flashed in him: "Can her convictions not be my convictions now?..."*

While compressing a large and complex novel into a few pages oversimplifies the spiritual struggle at the heart of the book, even through a brief retelling one can understand how Sonya's wisdom and love are enough to bring about Raskolnikov's conversion. More than any other person, she helps him understand that there is no alternative to confession and repentance. With these, the doors of the kingdom of God can open even for a man in prison who has committed one of the worst of sins. For the first time since childhood, Raskolnikov experiences inner freedom even though he has seven more years to serve.

The Brothers Karamazov, Dostoevsky's last novel, provides the author with another opportunity to explore the themes of sin and repentance, doing so on an even larger canvas than *Crime and Punishment*. Again the pivotal event is murder—an act of patricide by one of the sons of Fyodor Karamazov, a jeering, cynical man of unbridled lust and greed.

What we are starkly confronted with in the Karamazov brothers are very different human types.

There is Alyosha, the youngest, who has miraculously emerged from the moral squalor of his father's home with a purity of heart and compelling directness most people relinquish in adolescence. This is due in great measure to vivid memories of his mother, who before her early death held him in her arms before her icon of the Mother of God and the Christ Child, praying with tears for Alyosha's protection.

In the period described in the novel, Alyosha has become a novice at the local monastery, assigned to care for Fr. Zosima, a saintly monk who hears the confessions of countless pilgrims.[4] The Christ-like Alyosha is able to visit his father and listen to him ridicule Christianity in general and monastic life in particular without rising to the bait. He is one of the rarities in the human race who has no need to defend himself or his faith.

Then there is Ivan Karamazov with his diamond-hard intellect, a scholar with acute but abstracted analytical powers, who seems to be seeing the earth and its people not from where he stands but as if he were watching by telescope from the moon. He is an expert on religion, especially Orthodox Christianity, and his widely read essays are even admired by the monks at the local monastery. They assume he is a believer, yet in fact Ivan is an atheist, rejecting God so long as there is a single child suffering from incurable illness. He is the sort of atheist who is so obsessed with the God to whom he objects and against whom he revolts that he is as God-haunted as the devout Alyosha. God is for Ivan a problem of the mind, for Alyosha a presence in the heart. Alienated Ivan is among those laying the foundations for the terrifying revolution to come only a few decades later—one of those idealists who hope, as Fr. Zosima says, "to make a just order for themselves but, having rejected Christ, will end by drenching the earth with blood."

In the eldest brother, Dimitri, we meet a poetic, impulsive young man who has inherited his father's sensuality but not his greed or cunning. He is passionately in love with Grushenka, a capricious and manipulative local beauty—a woman who has also caught the eye of the elder Karamazov, so that we find father and son competing with each other for her attention, with the father having the advantage of wealth, the son the advantage of youth. Dimitri is an image of the tragic sinner Christ loves and readily forgives in response to the tiniest gesture of repentance. He is someone who might bathe Christ's feet with his tears. "Lord, I am loathsome," Dimitri cries out, "but I love you! If you send me to hell, even there will I love you."

Finally there is a fourth son, Smerdyakov, son of a simple-minded girl who hardly knew her name, fathered by Fyodor Karamazov when he happened upon Lizaveta one night and raped her. He never confessed his deed and thus never acknowledged Smerdyakov as his son, but following Lizaveta's death in childbirth, he allowed his servant Grigory and his wife to care for the boy, who grew up to become another of his father's servants. The bitter and withdrawn Smerdyakov has known even less love than the legitimate sons of Karamazov.

By the time the elder Karamazov is murdered, we know the brothers well enough to understand that each of them except Alyosha had a homicidal motive, and understand why it is that even Alyosha feels implicated in his father's murder, for he has learned from Fr. Zosima that "each is guilty of everything before everyone, and I most of all."

Finally Dimitri is accused and arrested on the basis of circumstantial evidence. "I am not guilty of my father's blood," declares Dimitri when charged, yet he concedes that his arrest is just spiritually. "I accept punishment not because I killed him, but because I wanted to kill him, and might well have killed him...." Only later does it become clear who really committed the act and how cunningly it was planned.

The reader also comes to understand that Ivan, though he did not commit the murder, is the crime's intellectual author. It was Ivan who convinced the murderer that, as there is no God, there is no sin. Now he discovers that ideology can be as deadly as an axe.

In one of the pivotal moments in the book, we find Alyosha talking with Ivan, now on the verge of madness, about the huge guilt Alyosha senses has taken hold of his brother. Alyosha suddenly turns to Ivan and says: "It was *not you* who killed father. ... You've accused yourself and confessed to yourself that you and you alone are the murderer. But it was not you who killed him, you are mistaken, the murderer was not you, do you hear, it was not you! God has sent me to tell you that."

Alyosha does not mean that Ivan is blameless in their father's death. In assuring Ivan that it was "not you," Alyosha wants his brother to understand that what he has done was the result of a demonic spirit at work within him rather than an action of his essential self. Should Ivan confuse the evil he has done with his deepest self, he will have damned himself and may never find his way out of the despair that results. Alyosha's message is a desperate effort to save Ivan's sanity and soul.

Demonic possession is a theme that Dostoevsky explored in *Demons* (a title sometimes translated as *The Possessed),* yet in this novel we meet no demons as such—only people possessed by radical ideas and ideologies. Demons become visible, writes Dostoevsky translator Richard Pevear, "only in distortions of the human image, the human countenance, and their force is measurable only by the degree of the distortion."[5]

The demons in Dostoevsky's novels operate via all the "isms" that flooded across Russia in the nineteenth century: idealism, rationalism, empiricism, materialism, utilitarianism, positivism, anarchism, socialism, and, common to them all, nihilism and atheism. Demons—invisible spirits serving Satan, the father of lies —discovered that many nineteenth-century intellectuals were more vulnerable to idealistic theories and slogans than to wealth or other traditional temptations that had worked so well with their parents. Evil ideologies invade a person, pervert him, gradually driving him to crime, insanity, or both. "It was not you who ate the idea," says one of the novel's principal figures, Pyotr Verkhovensky, "but the idea ate you."

"If we call Satan the father of lies, I think we begin to understand that evil is rooted in untruth, denial of the Truth, in deception," writes my friend Alice Carter:

> *Denial of Christ is denial of Truth, to deny His Resurrec-*
> *tion propels us into sin—sin which is the only response*
> *to seeing death as the end. If death is the end, attention*
> *to my biological needs is my first priority: my needs over*
> *everyone else. Any injustice, any crime can be tolerated*
> *and is really unavoidable, in this perception. My survival*
> *is first. The end justifies the means. And in a world with-*
> *out God, as Dostoevsky tells us, anything is possible,*
> *everything is permitted. What can prevent our murderous*
> *actions from overwhelming and destroying the earth?*[6]

Dostoevsky was no Manichean envisioning God and Satan as equally matched warring twins. His experiences while a prisoner had shown him that evil was not on an equal footing with good, that demons are capable only of destruction, not creation. Since we are made in God's image, evil can never be the essence of any person, even the most damaged, the most sinful, the most possessed. However weakened by habitual sin, each person re-tains to the last breath the freedom to turn from evil, to confess and repent. "Never confuse the person, formed in the image of God, with the evil that is in him, because evil is but a chance misfortune, illness, a devilish reverie," said Dostoevsky's con-temporary, St. John of Kronstadt. "But the very essence of the person is the image of God, and this remains in him despite every disfigurement."

Coping with disaster in his own life, Dostoevsky came to re-alize that God is both our private salvation and the only source of social cohesion. We live a different life if we know we are made by God, bear the Divine image, and that each of us is—and all of us are—accountable to God. To deny God is a form of suicide and at the same time the cause of social disintegration and mass murder.

In place of demonic ideas and ideologies, there is the reality of God's creation and of the person. There is the saving mystery of beauty. Thus we find Dostoevsky's heroes in sacramental moments kissing the earth and watering it with their tears. This is what Sonya proposed that Raskolnikov do at the four crossroads and what Alyosha did after the death of his saintly mentor, Fr. Zosima:

He did not stop on the porch, either, but went quickly down the steps. Filled with rapture, his soul yearned for freedom, space, vastness. Over him the heavenly dome, full of quiet, shining stars, hung boundlessly. From the zenith to the horizon the still-dim Milky Way stretched its double strand. Night, fresh and quiet, almost unstirring, enveloped the earth. The white towers and golden domes of the church gleamed in the sapphire sky. The luxuriant autumn flowers in the flowerbeds near the house had fallen asleep until morning. The silence of the earth seemed to merge with the silence of the heavens, the mystery of the earth touched the mystery of the stars.... Alyosha stood gazing and suddenly, as if he had been cut down, threw himself to the earth.

He did not know why he was embracing it, he did not try to understand why he longed irresistibly to kiss it, to kiss all of it, but he was kissing it, weeping, sobbing, and watering it with his tears, and he vowed ecstatically to love it, to love it unto ages of ages. "Water the earth with the tears of your joy, and love those tears ..." rang his soul. What was he weeping for? Oh, in his rapture he wept even for the stars that shone on him from the abyss, and "he was not ashamed of this ecstasy." It was as if threads from all those innumerable worlds of God all came together in his soul, and it was trembling all over, "touching other worlds." He wanted to forgive everyone and for everything, and to ask forgiveness, oh, not for himself! but for all and for everything, "as others are asking for me," rang in his soul.

TOOLS FOR EXAMINING CONSCIENCE

Christians live not only from Sunday to Sunday, and throughout the year from Pascha to Pascha, we live from liturgy to liturgy, from eucharist to eucharist, from communion to communion. Our lives are measured and tested by this sacred event. All that we are and do finds its beginning and end, its meaning, purpose and fulfillment in God's gift of holy communion through Christ and the Spirit in the Church.

—Fr. Thomas Hopko[1]

From the first century, attending the liturgy and receiving communion on Sundays and principal feast days has been at the heart of Christian life, the event that gives life a eucharistic dimension and center point. But communion—receiving Christ into ourselves—can never be routine, never something we deserve no matter what the condition of our life may be. For example, Christ solemnly warns us against approaching the altar if we are in a state of enmity with anyone. He tells us, "Leave your gift there at the altar, go first and be reconciled with your brother..." (Mt 5:23). In one of the parables, he describes a person who is ejected from the wedding feast because he isn't wearing a wedding garment: his tattered clothing is a metaphor for living a life which reduces conscience to rags (Mt 22:1-14).

Receiving Christ in communion during the liturgy is the keystone of *living* in communion—with God, with people, and with creation. Christ teaches us that love of God and love of neighbor sum up the Law. One way of describing a serious sin is to say it is any act which breaks our communion with God and with our neighbor.

It is for this reason that examination of conscience—if necessary, going to confession—is part of preparation for communion. This is an ongoing process of trying to see my life and actions with clarity and honesty—to look at myself, my choices, and my direction as known by God. The examination of conscience is an occasion not only to recall any serious sins committed since my last confession but, in Dorothy Day's words, an opportunity to notice "even the beginnings of sins against charity, chastity, sins of distraction, sloth or gluttony."

In a treatise on love, St. Maximus the Confessor (580–662), one of the principal theologians of the first millennium, issues a warning not to neglect attention to conscience:

> *Do not treat the conscience with contempt, for it always advises you to do what is best. It sets before you the will of God and the angels; it frees you from the secret defilements of the heart; and when you depart this life, it grants you the gift of intimacy with God.*[2]

Maximus—whose own fidelity to conscience resulted in torture and the cutting off of his tongue and right hand in the last year of his long life—describes conscience as an intimate friend always advising us to do what is best, revealing God's will and freeing us from the influence of our own flawed reasonings and "passions," as the Church Fathers refer to destructive obsessions. Conscience is that which opens the door to communion with God, guiding us to participate in God's perfection.

The education of conscience, writes Maximus, involves the acquisition of virtues (from the Latin word for strength):

*He who has succeeded in attaining the virtues and is en-
riched with spiritual knowledge sees things clearly in
their true nature. Consequently, he both acts and speaks
with regard to all things in a manner which is fitting,
and he is never deluded. For according to whether we
use things rightly or wrongly we become either good or
bad.*[3]

What is conscience that one can examine it? The word de-
rives from a Greek verb meaning "to have common knowledge"
or "to know with" someone, a concept that led to the idea of bearing witness concerning someone, especially yourself. Conscience
came to mean an inner faculty that guides us in making choices
which align us with God's will and which accuses us when we
break communion with God and with our neighbor.

Conscience is a reflection of the divine image at the core of
each person. "It may be considered a function of our nature,
which itself is good, even though, as 'fallen,' it is subject to the
corrupting influence of sin," writes Fr. John Breck, an Orthodox
theologian. "The conscience, nevertheless, is either developed or
undeveloped, that is, it reflects the divine image with greater or
lesser degrees of faithfulness and fullness."

Fr. John continues:

*The education of conscience is acquired in large mea-
sure through immersing ourselves in the ascetic tradition
of the Church: its life of prayer, sacramental and liturgical celebration, and scripture study. The education of
our conscience also depends upon our acquiring wisdom
from those who are more advanced than we are in faith,
love, and knowledge of God. In our day there is a tragic
lack of spiritual elders (such as the nineteenth century
Russian* startsi) *whose own life and experience have
brought them to a height of wisdom that is essential for
the perfection of the conscience. For the most part, we*

have to rely upon the written tradition of the Church:
scriptures, liturgy, and lives of the saints.[4]

The final document issued by the Second Vatican Council, the Constitution on the Church in the Modern World, offers a definition of conscience that stresses natural law—an innate capacity that each person possesses to distinguish good from evil:

In the depths of his conscience, each person detects a
law which he does not impose upon himself, but which
holds him to obedience. Always summoning each person
to love good and avoid evil, the voice of conscience when
necessary speaks to the heart more specifically: do this,
shun that. For we have in our hearts a law written by
God; to obey it is the very dignity of the human being;
according to it we will be judged. Conscience is our most
secret core and sanctuary. There each person is alone
with God whose voice echoes in his depths. In a wonder-
ful manner conscience reveals that law which is fulfilled
by love of God and neighbor. In fidelity to conscience,
Christians are joined with the rest of mankind in the
search for truth and for the genuine solution of the nu-
merous problems which arise in the lives of individuals
and from social relationships. Hence, the more right con-
science holds sway, the more persons and groups turn
aside from blind choice and strive to be guided by objec-
tive norms of morality. Conscience frequently errs from
individual ignorance without losing its dignity. The same
cannot be said for a person who cares little for truth and
goodness, or for conscience which by degrees grows
practically sightless as a result of habitual sin.[5]

"Hearing conscience" is how we speak of hearing God, but hearing God is no easy thing. Consider the story of the prophet Elijah waiting to hear God speak to him.

> *And behold, the Lord passed by, and a great and strong*
> *wind rent the mountains, and broke in pieces the rocks*
> *before the Lord, but the Lord was not in the wind; and*
> *after the wind an earthquake, but the Lord was not in the*
> *earthquake; and after the earthquake a fire, but the Lord*
> *was not in the fire; and after the fire a still small voice.*
> *And when Elijah heard it, he wrapped his face in his*
> *mantle and went out and stood at the entrance of the*
> *cave. And behold, there came a voice to him, and said,*
> *"What are you doing here, Elijah?"* (1 Kings 19:11-12)

Because conscience is a still small voice, it often takes a deep interior silence to hear it and careful discernment to distinguish that voice from our own wishes, compulsions, or ruinous urges. From time to time we hear of people committing murder or other sins who insist it was all because of an unrelenting inner voice that became "God" in their minds. It is unfortunately no rare thing to confuse angelic and demonic inner voices.

Conscience is God's whispering voice within us calling us to a way of life that reveals God's presence and urges us to refuse actions that destroy community and communion.

KEY ELEMENTS IN CONFESSION

Fr. Alexander Schmemann provided this summary of the three key areas of confession:

Relationship to God:
Questions on faith itself, possible doubts or deviations, inattention to prayer, neglect of liturgical life, fasting, etc.

Relationship to one's neighbor:
Basic attitudes of selfishness and self-centeredness, indifference to others, lack of attention, interest, love. All acts of actual of-

fense—envy, gossip, cruelty, etc.—must be mentioned and, if needed, their sinfulness shown to the penitent.

Relationship to one's self:
Sins of the flesh with, as their counterpart, the Christian vision of purity and wholesomeness, respect for the body as an icon of Christ, etc. Abuse of one's life and resources, absence of any real effort to deepen life; abuse of alcohol or other drugs; cheap idea of "fun," a life centered on amusement, irresponsibility, neglect of family relations, etc.

TOOLS OF SELF-EXAMINATION

In the struggle to hear conscience's quiet voice, we have tools that can assist us, resources that help both in the formation and the examination of conscience. Among these are the Ten Commandments, the Beatitudes, and various prayers, as well as lists of questions written by experienced confessors.

The Ten Commandments

The ten commandments were given to Moses on Mount Sinai (see Ex 20 and Deut 5) and have since become a basic point of reference for all who depend on the Bible. Few biblical texts have been so influential. The decalogue will always provide a useful framework for reviewing one's life.

You shall have no gods other than me. What was unique to the Jewish people, given to them to give to the world, was the revelation of there being only one God. This was also the unveiling of the principle of oneness within creation and the oneness of the human family. In the ancient world, people believed in many gods, great ones and lesser ones, some as local as a particular hill or tree. The Jews, having been enslaved in Egypt, were familiar with images of half-animal deities and inevitably had been influenced by Egyptian religious beliefs. Their long sojourn in the desert was not only a round-about journey away from Egypt and toward a promised land, but a slow shedding of attitudes and beliefs acquired in Egypt.

Questions to consider: Our own world, with its complex mixture of ideas, philosophies, religions, addictions, and obsessions, has much in common with the ancient world that surrounded the Jews and later the first Christians. Many pre-Christian religious beliefs are again being heavily promoted—multiple deities, reincarnation, pantheism, astrology, magic, witchcraft. In addition, there is the factor of a quasi-religious reverence toward science which in turn can promote a narrowly materialistic idea of existence. To what extent have I allowed values, habits, opinions, and doctrines that surround me to undermine a God-centered life and faith? Is there more than one God in my life?

You shall not make idols for yourselves. The second commandment is linked with the first. Because there is only one God, we must never worship false gods or representations of them. We are obliged to be careful that nothing takes the place of God in our lives.

Questions to consider: Idolatry is allowing anything other than God to become the axis on which life turns. So many things can take the place of God in one's life: property, social status, sports, diet, health, politics, causes, ideologies, tribe, clan, family, nationality. Are there objects or passions in my life that have become all-important? Pride makes a god of myself. Is it me that I worship? Greed makes a god of money. Is my attitude toward money and what it can buy a form of worship? Sensuality makes a god of the body. Do I worship my body? Whatever is loved, feared, delighted in, or depended on more than God has become a god in our lives.

You shall not use the name of the Lord your God in vain. Orthodox Jews are so sensitive to the Divine Name that it is never spoken aloud, while in writing the vowels are left out (G-d). Thus, Jews to this day bear witness to the veneration that should always mark one's attitude toward our Creator.

Questions to consider: Living as we do in a culture which often uses God's name in vain, it is no easy thing to avoid the irreverent use of the Divine Name. The principle of careful use of names also extends into our relations with the people around us. Do I regard God's name as holy? Do I speak of God with care and in an appropriate way? Do I discredit God's name by the way I live?

Keep the Sabbath day holy. Creation is portrayed in the Book of Genesis as a seven-stage process described figuratively as seven days—six days of labor, then a day of rest. The seventh day of the week is set aside for participation in God's tranquility. No other commandment in the Bible is mentioned so often as this one. The obligatory seventh day of rest is a day "to be kept holy." The injunction applies not only to oneself but also to servants as well as any laboring animals one has charge over.

Questions to consider: This is a commandment strictly limiting my busyness, yet I find myself in a culture which has no day or even hour of rest. It is extremely difficult not to be drawn into the surrounding restlessness. In what ways do I try to keep the Sabbath holy? In what ways am I failing?

Honor your father and mother. The first four commandments have to do with our relationship with God, the six that follow with the people around us. The first of the social commandments concerns those who brought us into this world, cared for us as we were growing up, and still play a role in our lives. It is not a commandment that prohibits disagreeing with parents or being blind to their faults and sins. Rather, it obligates us to take note of all that is admirable about them, to respect them, to help and care for them when help and care are needed.

Questions to consider: The fact that such a commandment exists reveals that it has always been a temptation for children to turn a blind or contemptuous eye toward their parents. An example is related by Jesus in his story of the prodigal son, but finally the son repents of his selfishness and begs his father's forgiveness. Many parents have in various ways failed in their responsibility to their children, but even in such cases children are not excused from responsibility for their parents. Have I been willing to forgive my parents for their failures? Have I made my parents aware that I am grateful for all they did on my behalf? Do I pray for them? Have I been ready to help them when help was needed?

Do not kill. Each commandment has generated controversy, none more so than the sixth commandment, with its absolute condemnation of killing. The commandment also bars abortion and the killing of the aged and handicapped.[6] No commandment has been more dramatically and tragically violated. Killing has been a common human activity ever since Cain murdered his brother Abel. Those martyred in the early Church included soldiers who, having been baptized, refused to kill. Yet there have been bishops, priests, and theologians who have spoken and acted as if there were no sixth commandment or as if the sixth commandment had only to do with private rather than collective activity.

Questions to consider: There are many ways to kill or participate in killing. Have I directly or indirectly caused another person's death? Do I sometimes behave in a way—for example, in the way I drive—that endangers the lives of others? Do I neglect opportunities to help those whose lives are in danger? Do I reverence the human being at each stage of life, from within the womb to old age? The poet William Blake wrote the disturbing line: "Better to murder an infant in its crib than to nurse an unfulfillable desire." Have I become a murderer in my imagination? Do I enjoy imagining the death of certain persons or groups of people? Killing is not only a private but also a societal activity in which relatively few individuals are required to do the actual killing or to enforce policies (economic sanctions, for example) that are bound to cause deaths, chiefly among the poorest, most defenseless, and least guilty members of the targeted country. To what extent am I cooperating with killing done collectively?

Do not commit adultery. Sexual infidelity in marriage has always been regarded as one of the gravest sins by the Church, as it was by the Jews who received the Law. The commandment not only has to do with sexual sins against marriage but also implicitly condemns any actions that damage marriage.

Questions to consider: There probably hasn't been a harder time to live a committed married life since the decadent period of the Roman Empire. We live in a culture in which sexual promiscuity is avidly promoted in ways the Romans of Caligula's generation could hardly imagine. Many films, television dramas, and novels present adultery and casual sex as normal and even admirable. Those who encourage sexual abstinence among the unmarried are regarded as old-fashioned, unrealistic enemies of happiness and freedom. Chastity and modesty are ridiculed. Do I try to protect myself from pornography and any form of propaganda or entertainment that undermines living chastely? If married, am I a faithful spouse? If unmarried, am I chaste? Am I an adulterer in my fantasies?

Do not steal. We are not allowed to take what we haven't been given, earned, or paid for. We are obliged not only to respect the property of others but also not to steal from ourselves by using our money and property in immoral ways. The rich are forbidden to steal from the poor through structures of oppression and injustice.

Questions to consider: Trust is built into every social and work situation. There is always the possibility of stealing with little or no risk of being caught. Co-workers may even resent the person who fails to "take advantage" of opportunities to steal or cheat. Am I honest in claims I make for repayment of expenses? Have I returned to others what they have loaned to me? I need to consider not only personal theft but also large political and economic structures that methodically and ruthlessly create destitution among some so that others might have wealth. Am I complicit in social structures that impoverish others?

Do not bear false witness. We are forbidden to lie. To put it positively, God commands that each of us tell the truth. A healthy community depends on truthful people. "Speak the truth and shame the devil," says an old proverb. My wife made a screensaver of the message: "Tell the truth. Don't be afraid."

Questions to consider: The lives and well-being of others depend on our being truthful. The commandment goes beyond honest testimony about others; it requires us not to speak falsely in any matter, not to deceive, not to hide the truth, not to gossip, not to unjustly damage the reputation of others. I am meant to be my neighbor's ally, not his or her enemy. Have I lied? Have I misled? Have I deceived? Have I sought ways to undermine someone else's reputation? Have I been truthful in making known my Christian faith to others? Have I objected to jokes that dehumanize or denigrate others? Or have I adapted myself to please others, to say what they want to hear rather than what I believe is true?

Do not covet what belongs to others. The final commandment has to do with lust for both things and people. Theft, adultery, violence, and war begin with coveting.

Questions to consider: It is a never-ending struggle to learn to look at things and people without wanting to possess them. Summarizing the way to live in the kingdom of God, Christ called on his followers to be poor in spirit. This is an attitude of *not* wanting rather than wanting. But we live in a society that constantly seeks to excite greed and to convince us that there is no such thing as having enough. In the world's history, no people have been under such constant stimulation to acquire more. Am I longing for things I don't need? Do I set limits on the ways I will use my resources so that my responsibility to others isn't derailed by my insistence on satisfying my own appetites first? What am I doing, through prayer and daily effort, to become less covetous?

The Beatitudes

Moses received the Ten Commandments on Mount Sinai, a fortress of stone in the barren wilderness east of Egypt. The Commandments of Blessedness, as the Russians call the Beatitudes, were taught by Christ in another high place, a towering hill near the Galilean lakeside town of Capernaum, an ideal place for a large gathering. Moses had to hide in the cleft of a rock to endure proximity to the glory of God, but on the Mount of the Beatitudes, God showed himself as the Son of Man. On Sinai, only Moses was permitted to come near, while in Galilee, anyone who was curious was welcome to see and listen.

These first verses of the Sermon on the Mount are a brief summary of the entire Gospel. The eight Beatitudes provide another way of examining conscience. Each Beatitude reveals an aspect of being in union with God.[7]

Blessed are the poor in spirit, for theirs is the kingdom of heaven. This is the essential first step. There is no other starting point for the rungs that follow. In a sense, the other Beatitudes are all contained in the first. Poverty of spirit is my awareness that I need God's help and mercy more than anything else. It is knowing that I cannot save myself, that neither money nor power will spare me from suffering and death, and that no matter what I achieve and acquire in this life, it will be far less than I want if I let my acquisitive capacity get the upper hand. This is the blessing of knowing that even what I have is not mine. It is living free of the domination of fear. While the exterior forms of poverty vary from person to person and even from year to year in a particular life, depending on one's vocation and special circumstances, all who live this Beatitude are seeking with heart and soul to live God's will rather than their own. Christ's mother is the paradigm of poverty of spirit in her unconditional assent to the will of God: "May it be done to me according to your word" (Lk 1:38). Similarly, at the marriage feast at Cana, she says to those waiting on the tables: "Do whatever he tells you" (Jn 2:5). Whoever lives by these words is poor in spirit.

Questions to consider: We are bombarded by advertisements, constantly reminded of the possibility of having things and of indulging all sorts of curiosities and temptations. The simple goal of poverty of spirit seems more remote than the moons of Neptune. Am I regularly praying that God will give me poverty of spirit? When tempted to buy things I don't need, do I pray for strength to resist? Do I keep the Church fasts that would help strengthen my capacity to live this Beatitude? Do I really seek to know and embrace God's will in my life? Am I willing to be seen as odd or stupid by those whose lives are dominated by values opposing the Beatitudes?

Blessed are they who mourn, for they shall be comforted. Ours is a society in which one can't go far without a smile. If we were looking for an up-to-date slogan to stamp on our money, perhaps it would be "Have a nice day." It certainly wouldn't be "Blessed are they who mourn." Mourning is cut from the same cloth as poverty of spirit. Without poverty of spirit, I am forever on guard to keep what I have for myself, and to keep me for myself, or for that small circle of people whom I regard as mine. A consequence of poverty of spirit is becoming vulnerable to the pain and losses of others, not only those whom I happen to know and care for, but also those who are strangers to me. "When we die," said Saint John Climacus, the seventh-century abbot of Saint Catherine's monastery near Mount Sinai, "we will not be criticized for having failed to work miracles. We will not be accused of having failed to be theologians or contemplatives. But we will certainly have to explain to God why we did not mourn unceasingly."[8]

Questions to consider: Do I weep with those who weep? Have I mourned those in my own family who have died? Do I open my thoughts and feelings to the suffering and losses of others? Do I try to make space in my mind and heart for the calamities in the lives of others who may be far away and neither speak my language nor share my faith?

Blessed are the meek, for they shall inherit the earth. Meekness is often confused with weakness, yet a meek person is neither spineless nor cowardly. Understood biblically, meekness is making choices and exercising power with a divine rather than social reference point. Meekness is the essential quality of the human being in relationship to God. Without meekness, we cannot align ourselves with God's will. In place of humility we prefer pride—pride in who we are, pride in doing as we please, pride in what we've achieved, pride in the national or ethnic group to which we happen to belong. Meekness has nothing to do with blind obedience or social conformity. Meek Christians do not allow themselves to be dragged along by the tides of political power. Such rudderless persons have cut themselves off from their own conscience, God's voice in their hearts, and thrown away their God-given freedom. Meekness is an attribute of following Christ no matter what risks are involved.

Questions to consider: When I read the Bible or writings of the saints, do I consider the implications for my own life? When I find what I read at odds with the way I live, do I allow the text to challenge me? Do I pray for God's guidance? Do I seek help with urgent questions in confession? Do I tend to make choices and adopt ideas that will help me fit into the group I want to be part of? Do I fear the criticism or ridicule of others for my efforts to live a Gospel-centered life? Do I listen to others? Do I tell the truth even in difficult circumstances?

Blessed are they who hunger and thirst for righteousness, for they shall be satisfied. In his teaching about the Last Judgment, Christ speaks of hunger and thirst: "I was hungry and you gave me food, I was thirsty and you gave me something to drink" (Mt 25:35). To hunger and thirst for something is not a mild desire but a desperate craving. Our salvation hinges on our caring for the least person as we would for Christ himself. To hunger and thirst for righteousness means to urgently desire that which is honorable, right, and true. A righteous person is a right-living person, living a moral, blameless life, right with both God and neighbor.

A righteous social order would be one in which no one is abandoned or thrown away, in which people live in peace with God, with each other, and with the world God has given us.

Questions to consider: Does it disturb me that I live in a world which in many ways is the opposite of the kingdom of heaven? When I pray "your kingdom come, your will be done on earth as it is in heaven," am I praying that my own life might better reflect God's priorities? Who is "the least" in my day-to-day world? Do I try to see Christ's face in him or her?

Blessed are the merciful, for they shall be shown mercy. One of the perils of pursuing righteousness is that one can become self-righteous. Thus, the next rung of the ladder of the Beatitudes is the commandment of mercy. This is the quality of self-giving love, of gracious deeds done for those in need. Twice in the Gospels Christ makes his own the words of the Prophet Hosea: "I desire mercy, not sacrifice (Hos 6:6; Mt 9:13, 12:7). We witness mercy in event after event in the New Testament account of Christ's life—forgiving, healing, freeing, correcting, even repairing the wound of a man injured by Peter in his effort to protect Christ and promising paradise to the criminal being crucified next to him. Again and again Christ declares that those who seek God's mercy must pardon others. The principle is included in the only prayer Christ taught his disciples, "Forgive us our debts as we forgive our debtors." He calls on his followers to love their enemies and to pray for them. The moral of the parable of the Good Samaritan is that a neighbor is a person who comes to the aid of a stranger in need (Lk 10:29-37). While denouncing hypocrisy and warning the merciless that they are condemning themselves to hell, in no passage in the Gospel do we hear Christ advocating anyone's death. At the Last Judgment Christ receives into the kingdom of heaven those who were merciful. He is Mercy itself.

Questions to consider: When I see a stranger in need, how do I respond? Is Christ's mercy evident in my life? Am I willing to extend forgiveness to those who seek it? Am I generous in sharing my time and material possessions with those in need? Do I pray for my enemies? Do I try to assist them if they are in need? Have I been an enemy to anyone?

Mercy is more and more absent even in societies with Christian roots. In the United States, the death penalty has been reinstated in the majority of states and has the fervent support of many Christians. Even in the many countries that have abolished executions, the death penalty is often imposed on unborn children—abortion is hardly regarded as a moral issue. Concerning the sick, aged, and severely handicapped, "mercy" killing and "assisted suicide" are now phrases much in use. To what extent have I been influenced by slogans and ideologies that promote death as a solution and disguise killing as mercy? What am I doing to make my society more welcoming, more caring, more life-protecting?

Blessed are the pure of heart, for they shall see God. The brain has come up in the world while the heart has been demoted. The heart used to be widely recognized as the locus of God's activity within us, the hub of human identity and conscience, linked with our capacity to love, the core not only of physical but also of spiritual life—the ground zero of the human soul. In our brain-centered society, we ought to be scandalized that Christ didn't say, "Blessed are the pure in mind," or better yet, "Blessed are the brilliant in mind." Instead, he blessed purity of heart. The Greek word for purity, *katharos*, means spotless, stainless; intact, unbroken, perfect; free from adulteration or anything that defiles or corrupts. What, then, is a pure heart? A heart free of possessiveness, a heart capable of mourning, a heart that thirsts for what is right, a merciful heart, a loving heart, a heart not ruled by passions, an undivided heart, a heart aware of the image of God in others, a heart drawn to beauty, a heart conscious of God's presence in creation. A pure heart is a heart without contempt for others. "A person is truly pure of heart when he considers all human beings as good and no created thing appears impure or defiled to him," wrote Saint Isaac of Syria. Opposing purity of heart is lust of any kind—for wealth, for recognition, for power, for vengeance, for sexual exploits—whether indulged through action or imagination. Spiritual virtues that defend the heart are memory, awareness, watchfulness, wakefulness, attention, hope, faith, and love. A rule of prayer in daily life helps heal, guard, and unify the heart. "Always keep your mind collected in your heart," instructed the great teacher of prayer, Saint Theofan the Recluse. The Jesus Prayer—the Prayer of the Heart—is part of a tradition of spiritual life that helps move the center of consciousness from the mind to the heart. Purification of the heart is the striving to place under the rule of the heart the mind, which represents the analytic and organizational aspect of consciousness. It is the moment-to-moment prayerful discipline of seeking to be so aware of God's presence that no space is left in the heart for hatred, greed, lust, or vengeance. Purification of the heart is the lifelong struggle of seeking a more God-centered life, a heart illuminated with the presence of the Holy Trinity.

Questions to consider: Do I take care not to read or look at things that stir up lust? Do I avoid using words that soil my mouth? Am I attentive to beauty in people, nature, and the arts? Am I sarcastic about others? Is a rhythm of prayer part of my daily life? Do I prepare carefully for communion, never taking it for granted? Do I observe fasting days and seasons? Am I aware of and grateful for God's gifts?

Blessed are the peacemakers, for they will be called children of God. Christ is often called the Prince of Peace. His peace is not a passive condition—he blesses the *makers* of peace. The peacemaker is a person who helps heal damaged relationships. Throughout the Gospel we see Christ bestowing peace. In his final discourse before his arrest, he says to the Apostles: "Peace I leave with you, my peace I give to you. . . . Let not your hearts be troubled, neither let them be afraid" (Jn 14:27). After the Resurrection, he greets his followers with the words, "Peace be with you" (Lk 24:36; Jn 20:19). He instructs his followers that, on entering a house, their first action should be the blessing, "Peace be to this house" (Lk 10:5). Christ is at his most paradoxical when he says, "Do not think that I have come to bring peace on earth; I have not come to bring peace, but a sword" (Mt 10:34; note that a similar passage in Luke uses the word "division" rather than "sword"). Those who try to live Christ's peace may find themselves in trouble, as all those who have died a martyr's death bear witness. Sadly, for most of us, the peace we long for is not the kingdom of God but a slightly improved version of the world we already have. We would like to get rid of conflict without eliminating the spiritual and material factors that draw us into conflict. The peacemaker is a person aware that ends never stand apart from means: figs do not grow from thistles; neither is community brought into being by hatred and violence. A peacemaker is aware that all persons, even those who seem to be possessed by evil spirits, are made in the image of God and are capable of change and conversion.

Questions to consider: In my family, in my parish, and among my co-workers, am I guilty of sins which cause or deepen division and conflict? Do I ask forgiveness when I realize I am in the wrong? Or am I always justifying what I do, no matter what pain or harm it causes others? Do I regard it as a waste of time to communicate with opponents? Do I listen with care and respect to those who irritate me? Do I pray for the well-being and salvation of adversaries and enemies? Do I allow what others say or what the press reports to define my attitude toward those whom I have never met? Do I take positive steps to overcome division? Are there people I regard as not bearing God's image and therefore innately evil?

Blessed are they who are persecuted for the sake of righteousness, for theirs is the kingdom of heaven. Blessed are you when they insult you and persecute you and utter every kind of evil against you falsely because of me. Rejoice and be glad, for your reward will be great in heaven, for so men persecuted the prophets who were before you. The last rung is where the Beatitudes reach and pass beyond the cross. "We must carry Christ's cross as a crown of glory," wrote Saint John Chrysostom in the fourth century, "for it is by it that everything that is achieved among us is gained.... Whenever you make the sign of the cross on your body, think of what the cross means and put aside anger and every other passion. Take courage and be free in the soul."[9]

In the ancient world, Christians were persecuted chiefly because they were regarded as undermining the social order even though in most respects they were models of civil obedience and good conduct. But Christians abstained from the cult of the deified emperor, would not sacrifice to gods their neighbors venerated, and were notable for their objection to war or bloodshed in any form. It is easy to imagine that a community that lived by such values, however well-behaved, would be regarded as a threat by the government. "Both the Emperor's commands and those of others in authority must be obeyed if they are not contrary to the God of heaven," said Saint Euphemia in the year 303 during the reign of Diocletian. "If they are, they must not only be disobeyed; they must be resisted." Following torture, Saint Euphemia was killed by a bear—the kind of death endured by thousands of Christians well into the fourth century, though the greatest number of Christian martyrs belongs to the twentieth century. In many countries religious persecution continues.

Questions to consider: Does fear play a bigger role in my life than love? Do I hide my faith or live it in a timid, half-hearted way? When I am ordered to do something that conflicts with Christ's teaching, whom do I obey? Am I aware of those who are suffering for righteousness' sake in my own country and elsewhere in the world? Am I praying for them? Am I doing anything to help them?

The Last Judgment

Each time we examine our conscience, we are preparing for the Last Judgment: the final weighing up of each and every life at the end of history. It is an event that Christ describes in vivid terms:

When the Son of man comes in his glory, and all the angels with him, then he will sit on his glorious throne. Before him will be gathered all the nations, and he will separate them one from another as a shepherd separates the sheep from the goats, and he will place the sheep at his right hand, but the goats at the left. Then the King will say to those at his right hand, "Come, O blessed of my Father, inherit the kingdom prepared for you from the foundation of the world; for I was hungry and you gave me food, I was thirsty and you gave me drink, I was a stranger and you welcomed me, I was naked and you clothed me, I was sick and you visited me, I was in prison and you came to me." Then the righteous will answer him, "Lord, when did we see you hungry and feed you, or thirsty and give you drink? And when did we see you a stranger and welcome you, or naked and clothe you? And when did we see you sick or in prison and visit you?" And the King will answer them, "Truly, I say to you, as you did it to one of the least of these my brethren, you did it to me." Then he will say to those at his left hand, "Depart from me, you cursed, into the eternal fire prepared for the devil and his angels; for I was hungry and you gave me no food, I was thirsty and you gave me no drink, I was a stranger and you did not welcome me, naked and you did not clothe me, sick and in prison and you did not visit me." Then they also will answer, "Lord, when did we see you hungry or thirsty or a stranger or naked or sick or in prison, and did not minister to you?" Then he will answer them, "Truly, I say to you, as you did it not to one of the least of these, you did it not to me." And they will go away into eternal punishment, but the righteous into eternal life. (Mt 25:31-46)

Christ identifies himself with those in the most urgent conditions of need: the hungry, thirsty, naked, homeless, sick, and imprisoned. The lesson is simple. In responding to the desperate needs of others, we respond to him: "As you did to the least person, you did to me."

Dorothy Day often said, "Those who cannot see Christ in the poor are atheists indeed." St. John Chrysostom said it as well, linking Christ in the Eucharist with Christ hungry and naked outside the church:

> *Do you wish to honor the Body of the Savior? Do not despise it when it is naked. Do not honor it in church with silk vestments while outside it is naked and numb with cold. He who said, "This is my body," and made it so by his word, is the same who said, "You saw me hungry and you gave me no food. As you did it not to the least of these, you did it not to me." Honor him then by sharing your property with the poor. For what God needs is not golden chalices but golden souls.*[10]

It is not only in words that Christ identified with those who have nothing and are regarded with contempt. He was born in a stable because no better place was offered for his mother to give birth. As a child he was a refugee. Later in life he said, "Foxes have holes, and birds of the air have nests; but the Son of man has nowhere to lay his head" (Mt 8:20). He was imprisoned and died a criminal's death. Given all that, is it a surprise that God's hospitality to us is linked to our hospitality to those who have little or nothing? If we avoid Christ in the poor, we are avoiding the gate to heaven.

In addition to the corporal works of mercy of which Christ speaks in Matthew's Gospel, there are parallel spiritual works of mercy:

> *cautioning the sinner, instructing the ignorant, counseling the doubtful, comforting the sorrowful, bearing wrongs patiently, forgiving all injuries, praying for the living and the dead.*

Questions to consider: Do I help those in need of help? Do I avoid or ignore the poor? Do I assume the worst of beggars? Do I give to communities carrying out works of mercy or trying in other ways to alleviate suffering? Do I keep in mind that Christ is present in others, most of all in those lacking necessities? Do I look for opportunities to practice the corporal and spiritual works of mercy?

The Prayer of Ephraim the Syrian

There are numerous biblical passages that can serve as mirrors when considering one's spiritual health. In addition, there are many prayers that can help us examine basic questions. One of these, a short prayer written in the fourth century by Saint Ephraim the Syrian, is recited by Orthodox Christians every day throughout Lent:

> *O Lord and Master of my life, take from me the spirit of sloth, despair, lust for power and idle talk. But give to me, your servant, the spirit of chastity, humility, patience and love. O Lord and King, grant to me to see my own faults and not to condemn my brother and sister. For you are blessed unto the ages of ages.*

Reflect on the prayer phrase by phrase and let it question you.

O Lord and Master of my life

Who is Lord and master of my life? Me? God? The ideas, slogans, and choices of people around me?

take from me the spirit of sloth

"The spirit of sloth" refers to laziness, indolence, indifference, or forgetfulness. In a commentary on the prayer, Fr. Alexander

Schmemann regards sloth as the "basic disease...that strange
laziness that always pushes us down rather than up—which constantly convinces us that no change is possible and therefore de-
sirable. It is in fact a deeply rooted cynicism which to every spiritual challenge responds 'what for?' and makes our life one
tremendous spiritual waste."[11] Sloth, says Olivier Clément in another commentary, is "a kind of sleepwalking, whether expressed
in hyperactivity or in inertia."[12] How much of an effort do I make
in daily life to try to think of Christ and try to follow him? To be
aware of God's presence in people and in nature? To actively seek
the kingdom of God? To respond to God's grace?

despair

The word in question is sometimes translated from the Greek as
despondency or faint-heartedness. It also suggests discourage-
ment, being cowardly, an aversion to life—suicide of the soul. An
important icon shows Saint George in combat with a dragon. The
actual George, a martyr of the early Church, never saw a dragon
but battled against those fears which, unresisted, make one submit
to evil. Not to battle the dragons we meet in life is to submit to
despair, to give way to faint-heartedness. Am I easily discour-
aged? Do I surrender within myself when frightened? Am I cowardly in living my faith? Do I arm myself for spiritual combat
with a rule of prayer in my daily life?

lust for power

This is the spirit of self-importance, the religion of Me. The
spirit of domination was the third temptation to which Jesus was
subjected during his time of fasting in the wilderness. Christ dismissed Satan with the words, "The Lord your God shall you
worship and him alone shall you serve" (Mt 4:8-11). Lust for
power makes an idol of the self. Do I seek to control or manipu-
late others? To be feared by others? Do I want to have the last
word?

and idle talk

In a word, gossip. This is talk that attacks the social fabric much as termites attack the foundations of a wooden house. Idle talk refers to all chatter, not only mine but the empty chatter of others, including the chatter of television. The poet Carl Sandberg warns his daughter to be careful about what she says: "Words wear tall boots. They go marching off. You can't stop them when they're gone." Christ cautions us that we will render an account "for every careless word" we speak (Mt 12:36). Have I lied or gossiped? Have I maligned or slandered others? Have I cursed anyone? Have I become addicted to noise because I cannot bear silence?

But give to me, your servant, the spirit of chastity

The Greek word *sophrosini*, often translated as chastity, also means wholeness, self-control, sobriety, moderation, discretion, modesty, overcoming all passions that destroy life. To be chaste is to be pure in thought and conduct, to be free of addictions, to be in communion with God's purity. It is the wholeness of an interior innocence, a virginal freshness of soul. Chastity exists in marriage when there is an integration of desire in a personal relationship marked by self-giving love. A chaste person, notes Clément, is no longer fragmented. "If we usually mean by chastity the virtue opposed to sexual depravity," writes Fr. Alexander Schmemann, "it is because the broken character of our existence is nowhere better manifested than in sexual lust—the alienation of the body from the life and control of the spirit."[13] Do I realize my physical and spiritual life as one thing, not two? Have I used or regarded others as sexual objects? Have I damaged the spirit of chastity in myself by reading or looking at pornography? Have I dressed and behaved modestly?

humility

Humility is poverty of spirit and meekness. Humility inspires an attitude of listening and of seeking out those who can give good counsel. Humility welcomes correction. A humble person is not proud or arrogant. Humility is not the denial of my value as a human being but rather seeing myself in relationship to God. Humility results from being in a state of gratitude rather than envy, resentment, or bitterness. Do I boast about myself? Do I respect others? Do I listen with attention and a readiness to learn? Do I resent good advice? Do I accept correction with gratitude? Or do I defend myself even when I am in the wrong?

patience

Patience is calmly bearing or enduring delay, disappointment, pain, and sorrow. It is a deep confidence in God's providence and the willingness to persevere even in the face of loss and failure. Clément speaks of patience as an "interiorized monasticism."[14] It is not resignation but the awareness that truly Christ is risen from the dead and is with us moment to moment, no matter where we go or what we are enduring. Do I imagine I am alone? That I am God-forsaken? Do I resent delays? Do I give up when there are too many obstacles? Do I tend to do things in a hurry? Am I easily annoyed with others? Do I get angry when I don't get my way?

and love

Love is the quality most needed. In speaking of God, while no word is adequate, none is truer than to say that God is love. "God so loved the world that He sent his only begotten Son," writes Saint John (Jn 3:16). Love of its nature inspires whole-hearted giving, an eagerness to serve, care of words, humility, and patience. It is self-giving, even a death to self. We are taught by Christ not only to love our friends but also our enemies, for without love there is no way to overcome enmity, as he shows us with his own life. Much more than a sentiment, love is an attitude of caring for the well-being and salvation of others. Do I tend to put my needs and desires first? Do I pray for those I fear or hate?

Does it disturb me to think that a person I do not like is also God's child and bears the Divine Image? Do I look for ways to help others even if they are strangers?

O Lord and King, grant to me to see my own faults and not to condemn my brother and sister. For you are blessed unto the ages of ages.

Twice in this prayer God is addressed as Lord, once as Master, and once as King. This is Saint Ephraim's way of helping us address our Creator in a spirit of respect and obedience. It may not be our desire to serve others or put their needs before our own, but if this is what God asks of us, we work to convert ourselves to living as God wishes. We especially ask God to make us aware of our own faults and sins rather than judge others. After all, at the Last Judgment I will be judged for my own sins, not the sins others committed, except to the extent that others sinned because I sinned. Do I care more about what is wrong with other people than what is wrong with myself? Do I look down on those who appear to have an even less ordered life than mine? Do I regard myself as not so bad because there are others who are worse?

FINDING A CONFESSOR

Do not reveal your thoughts to everyone, but only to them that can save your soul.

—Saint Anthony the Great

Do not reveal your conscience to him to whom your heart is not well disposed.

—Saint Pimen the Great

There are occasional confessors who have access to unrevealed facts about penitents which they could have no usual way of knowing. The Holy Spirit allows them to see things which the penitent hasn't revealed. One such confessor was St. John Vianney—the Curé of Ars—who was ordained a priest despite misgivings regarding his limited academic ability. "Even more than learned priests, the Church needs holy priests," one of his sponsors argued. After some time spent assisting the pastor of his own parish, in 1825 he was sent to the remote French village of Ars-en-Dombes, an insignificant corner of the diocese, but for the curé, it was a doorway to heaven. So devoted was he to his 250 neighbors that it slowly dawned on them that their salvation was of the utmost importance to the humble priest who had come to care for them. Little by little they began coming to him for confession. The curé had a rare gift for discovering penitents' secrets and unspoken thoughts and clearing away obstacles in their relationship with God.

Word of the saintly curé spread. So many came to him for confession that he would often be in the confessional ten or twelve hours a day or more. Toward the end of his life, the railroad provided special trains to bring penitents to Ars. Having deserted from the army in his youth, he was amused when the emperor, Napoleon III, sent him the medal of the Legion of Honor. The curé refused to take it out of the box. "I don't know what I have done to deserve this except to be a deserter," he remarked.

A generation later, there was St. Amvrosy at the monastery in Optina, Russia. Over the years countless thousands came to Optina, many of them walking for days or even weeks to get there, to confess to him or seek his advice on marriages, disputes, or questions that were troubling them—the kinds of scenes Dostoevsky describes in the early pages of *The Brothers Karamazov*. Amvrosy's advice was often very simple. He might point out to someone obsessed with material needs "that we are pilgrims on this earth and that it befits us to enter the Kingdom of Heaven through many sorrows." It was a comment one could hear from any priest in Russia, yet there was something about Amvrosy's attention to the person he was addressing that often made it possible for the pilgrim, instead of dismissing the words as a cliché, to regard his life, priorities, and vocation in a transfigured light.[1]

God sends the occasional Curé of Ars and Staretz Amvrosy, but such saints of confession are rare. Perhaps a major part of their role is simply to inspire other priests to be better confessors and to renew our attention to the sacrament of confession.

Thinking you need a saint to hear your confession can be a barrier rather than an aid to spiritual growth. Fr. Alexis Vinogradov recalls how his father-in-law, the noted theologian and teacher Fr. Alexander Schmemann, once complained in his journal about seminary students who spend a lot of time searching for the perfect spiritual father. "He recalled that in his youth, when he needed a confessor, he would run like fire to the nearest priest, knowing that he needed to confess and knowing any priest was ordained to hear it. What mattered was his own need to confess, not the qualities of the priest. He likened this to the morning fog which awaits the sun to burn it off."

Yet at times one may have to look beyond the parish. As one experienced priest wrote me, a priest may be an excellent confessor for one person yet not at all well matched to another. "I see this all the time," he told me. "It's a mystery that comes with life in the body."

Some people are too eager to find the ideal spiritual father. One has to take care. As a deacon in our parish, John Sewter, wrote me recently:

I have observed in adult converts that, if and when they start trying to find their own special father confessor or spiritual father, there can be a conflict of interests. It can be good searching for someone who can help them grow spiritually. On the other hand, they are probably the worst persons to decide which confessor is really the best for them. Of course each person can get more out of confession if both parties are on the same wavelength, but often I see people shopping around, consciously or unconsciously, for someone who will agree with them, or at least go a long way with them in their own opinions. We cannot know within a short space of time if we have found the right confessor for ourselves, but only perhaps after several years experience and—hopefully—growth. This makes it almost impossible to give any directions to those who ask for advice on different confessors, except perhaps that it is essential for them to be on the same wavelength and understand each other.

A friend reminded me recently that the search for the "perfect" priest is like the search for the "perfect" parish. The perfect parish doesn't exist, but you can go to hell looking for it, refusing to be part of any parish made up of people who are as flawed as you are.

While confessor saints are rare, good confessors are common and usually near at hand. I'm not aware of ever having met a priest who was clairvoyant or possessed other astonishing spiritual gifts, but I have often encountered priests who listened in a way that helped me confess, perhaps even helped me realize what I actually needed to confess, before they recited the words that assured me of God's forgiveness. What good confessors have in common isn't their ability to instantly "read the souls" of those who come to them, but their capacity to inspire penitents to *want* to be seen and to reveal things about themselves which need to be confessed.

Usually your confessor is the priest who is closest, sees you most often, knows you and the circumstances of your life best: a priest of your parish. Do not be put off by your awareness of what you perceive as his relative youth, his personal shortcomings, or the probability that he possesses no rare spiritual gifts. Keep in mind that each priest goes to confession himself and may have more to confess than you do. You confess not to him but to Christ in his presence. He is the *witness* of your confession—you do not require and will never find a sinless person to be that witness. (The Orthodox Church tries to make this clear by having the penitent face not the priest but an icon of Christ.) What he says by way of advice can be remarkably insightful or brusque or seem to you a cliché and not very relevant, yet almost always there will be something helpful if only you are willing to hear it. Sometimes there is a suggestion or insight that becomes a turning point in your life. If he imposes a penance—normally increased prayer, fasting, and acts of mercy—it should be accepted meekly, unless there is something in the penance which seems to you a violation of your conscience or of the teaching of the Church as you understand it.

Don't imagine that a priest will respect you less for what you reveal to Christ in the priest's presence or imagine that he is carefully remembering all your sins. "Even a recently ordained priest will quickly find that he cannot remember 99 percent of what people tell him in confession," a priest in our parish told me. He said it is embarrassing to him that people expect him to remember what they told him in an earlier confession. "When they remind me, then sometimes I remember, but without a reminder, usually my mind is a blank. I let the words I listen to pass through me. Also, so much that I hear in one confession is similar to what I hear in other confessions—the confessions blur together. The only sins I easily remember are my own."

One priest mentioned his difficulties meeting the expectations that sometimes become evident in confession. "I am not a psychologist. I have no special gifts. I am just a fellow sinner trying to stay on the path."

A Russian priest said he almost always feels joy hearing confessions. "It is not that I am glad anyone has sins to confess but when you come to confession it means these sins are in your past, not your future. Confession marks a turning point and I am the lucky one who gets to watch people making that turn!"

But other priests find it hard and difficult work. Fr. Alexander Schmemann observed:

> *For each conscientious priest confession is without any doubt one of the most difficult and frustrating aspects of his ministry. It is here, on the one hand, that he encounters the only real object of his pastoral care: the human soul, man, as he stands sinful and miserable, before God. But it is here, on the other hand, that he realizes to what degree nominal Christianity has pervaded our Church life. The basic Christian notions of sin and repentance, reconciliation with God and renewal of life, seem to have become irrelevant. If the terms are still used, their meaning is certainly quite different from that on which our whole Christian faith is based.[2]*

Too often, Fr. Alexander noted, those who come to confession regard it as "counseling"—a meeting with "a supposedly wise and experienced advisor with ready answers to all human problems" rather than a dialogue between the person confessing and God.

"What helps a priest become a good confessor? If he has a good confessor himself, if he has a good wife or abbot," my friend Yves Dubois, priest of an Orthodox parish in Bath, England, tells me. "If he is surrounded by friends who tease him to make sure he does not become a guru, who make up a community around him where the atmosphere is healthy and where the community becomes itself a healthy regulator for the priest's and everyone's conscience."

He comments that the parish priest must be aware that there are those for whom any male presents difficulties as a confessor. "People with a painful relationship with their father may need someone other than a priest as their main contact, adviser, moral support in their parish community, and the parish priest must make himself small. The relationship may develop much later, but most probably needs to remain extremely light on a life-long basis."

Bishop Kallistos Ware, longtime professor at Oxford and confessor to many, emphasizes how important it is for a priest witnessing confessions to prefer questions to commands:

Fr. Sophrony of the monastery in Essex once told me about the approach of Saint Silouan of Mt. Athos towards those who came to him. He said that Staretz Silouan hardly ever told people exactly what to do, he hardly ever issued commands. Much more often, he would ask them questions—very carefully chosen questions, yes—but he didn't issue orders. He wanted people to think for themselves. If Staretz Silouan did give counsel in a more detailed way, he frequently began his sentences with the word, "If." In other words, he tried to help people see connections, to see that if they did one thing, then that would lead on to something else, so there is a chain of cause and effect within our spiritual lives. He tried to help people see how things hang together, how one thing leads to another. Still he left it to them to make up their own minds.

If somebody comes to me and just says, "Tell me what I should do," my response is, "That is not the real question. You can only discover what you should do if you look in a much more precise way at what the possi-

*bilities are and what the alternatives are. Then you can
begin to make a choice. But the question, just in the ab-
stract, 'What should I do?', is not yet ready for an answer." The spiritual father doesn't issue orders, he's not
a lawgiver. But he can, sometimes, help people to see
what the question is.*[3]

It shouldn't be hard to find a capable and conscientious priest
to hear your confession, but there has to be a word of warning.

Just as not every doctor is a good physician, not every priest
is a good confessor. Sometimes it happens that a priest, however
good his qualities in other respects, is a person best avoided in the
sacrament of confession. Unsuited or abusive priests are the ex-
ception, but their existence must be noted. God has given us freedom and provided each person with a conscience. It is not the role
of a priest to take the place of conscience or to become anyone's
drill sergeant. A good confessor will help us become better at
hearing conscience and becoming more free in an increasingly
God-centered life.

I've been fortunate. My worst experience of confession was-
n't that bad. I had recently been discharged from the Navy, was a
new addition to the Catholic Worker community in lower Manhattan, and was getting to know various city parishes. One Saturday
night it was an uptown Dominican parish. Inside the confessional,
I had started out with what were regarded as minor—venial—sins,
working my way toward more serious sins. The unseen priest
yelled at me, "Mortal sins first!" His irate voice seemed loud
enough to travel from one end of Manhattan island to the other.
More than thirty years later, his furious shout still reverberates in
my head. I finished my confession, very red-faced, but never returned for confession in that church in dread that I might discover
him on the other side of the grille and be yelled at again for failing
to confess in exactly the right way. I can easily imagine those for
whom such a confession might have been their last.

I've been in the Orthodox Church since 1988 and over the
years been to confession at Orthodox parishes in Holland, Bel-

gium, America, Britain, France, Russia, and Serbia. So far I have experienced only good and helpful confessions, but I know from others that there are Orthodox priests who are poor confessors. In Russia, there are occasional reports of ultra-fervent young priests here and there who were only children or in their teens when the Soviet era ended, yet today are as ready as Communist Party officials once were to tell others exactly what to think and do, eager to be the voice of conscience for others and to place penitents who come to them under their absolute domination. Russians sometimes describe such priests as "elders who have not yet grown a beard." (The "elder"—*staretz* in Russian—is the rare person who sees into the depths of a penitent's heart even before a word is said, like the aged monk Staretz Zosima in Dostoevsky's *The Brothers Karamazov*. Such a vocation is never aspired to, never claimed, and never comes in youth.) Occasionally one hears of similar would-be "elders" in other countries.

Priests who seek to deprive others of freedom are not a new problem. In his later life, Nikolai Gogol, the author of the comic masterpiece, *Dead Souls*, and some of the world's funniest short stories, fell under the damaging influence of a priest named Fr. Matthew Konstantinovsky, a man whose asceticism far surpassed that of many monks. Permanently fasting, Fr. Matthew drank no wine and ate no meat even on feast days, avoided and condemned all worldly pleasures, approved reading only the Bible, the writings of saints, and liturgical texts. He ordered Gogol to put aside his admiration for the poet Pushkin, whose gold watch had been left to Gogol. "Deny Pushkin! He was a sinner and a pagan!" Though none of Fr. Matthew's letters to Gogol survive, a letter he sent to a widow who sought his blessing for remarriage gives an impression of what he was like:

> *Do not trade God for the devil and the kingdom of heaven for this world. You will have one moment of pleasure here and then weep for all eternity. Do not enter into conflict with God; do not marry again. You know well that the Lord Himself requires you to struggle*

*against the flesh. Think of death, and it will be easier for
you to live. If you forget death, you will forget God. If
you adorn your soul here below with fasting and abstinence, it will be pure when it reaches the hereafter. You
know what to do in order to calm your passions: eat little
and as seldom as possible, avoid gluttony, give up tea,
drink cold water instead, with a piece of bread, and that
only when you need them. Sleep less, speak less, and
work more.*

It is not that Fr. Matthew's letter is completely lacking in useful advice. Fasting days and seasons have been part of Christian
life from the Church's first generations. Moderation is a virtue,
gluttony a vice. The remembrance of mortality can be life-giving,
so long as remembrance does not become obsession. It's possible
there were even good reasons to counsel this particular woman
against remarriage, though one has the impression that Fr. Matthew prefers a cold bed to a warm one. But, taken as a whole,
Fr. Matthew's voice is that of the Grand Inquisitor rather than
Christ's, a voice that resounds with condemnation rather than
mercy, rage rather than love, fear of life rather than gratitude. For
him what the Church asks of its members is not strict enough, the
Church's "narrow way" not narrow enough. By way of contrast,
consider the sensible advice to a penitent from a Russian saint
who heard thousands of confessions, Seraphim of Sarov: "Give
the spirit what is due to it and the body what it needs, so the body
can carry the spirit along the way of salvation.... In the spiritual
life do nothing beyond your strength but always take the middle
way, for this is the royal road."[4]

For people like Gogol, terrified of their own capacity to sin,
for whom Christ is overshadowed by the anti-Christ, a tyrannical
figure like Fr. Matthew can seem a rescuer. Thus, Fr. Matthew became the dominant figure in Gogol's life in its last stage, driving
the writer into an ever-deepening despair. At their last meeting,
the priest described the Last Judgment, stressing not Christ's
mercy but his mercilessness. Few would be spared, many would

be delivered to the torments of hell. Gogol at last begged him to stop. "Enough! I can't listen to you anymore! It's too awful."[5]

"He seems to have practiced on Gogol a kind of spiritual sadism," writes one of Gogol's biographers, Janko Lavrin. Under Fr. Matthew's influence, while in a state of semi-madness, Gogol burned the manuscript of the book he had been working on, a sequel to *Dead Souls,* plus other works in progress. Utterly dispirited, he died ten days later, in March 1852. He was only forty-two years old. A painting in Gogol's Moscow apartment (today a museum) shows the despondent writer feeding pages into a cast iron stove while Fr. Matthew looks on with a demonic gleam in his eye. It is an invented scene—Fr. Matthew was not present when Gogol destroyed his manuscripts—yet the image sums up the role the stern, disapproving confessor played in the tragic final weeks of Gogol's life.

There is a similar figure in the life of St. Elizabeth of Hungary, a woman the Church remembers especially for her tireless care of the poor. She too was confronted with a tyrannical priest, Master Conrad of Marburg, a former inquisitor who might have driven a more vulnerable person to despair. A queen who became a nun following her husband's death in 1225, Elizabeth was sometimes punished with slaps and blows by her confessor. He made her vow to obey him in every matter, great and small. After her husband's death, he sent away anyone who had been dear to her and strove to crush her will. "Conrad's policy of breaking rather than directing the will was not completely successful," note Herbert Thurston and Donald Attwater in their revision of *Butler's Lives of the Saints.* Referring to Conrad and his disciplinary methods, St. Elizabeth compares herself to sedge in a stream during flood-time: "The water bears it down flat, but when the rains have gone it springs up again, straight, strong and unhurt." She also compared herself to a snail "which withdraws into its shell when it is going to rain."[6]

Though not numerous, bullying priests still exist. One friend who belonged to a small American Orthodox mission parish wrote me: "Our priest was a convert and so was I. He had the conviction that he needed not just to hear confessions but insisted on being each person's 'spiritual father' in the monastic sense of the term. He insisted on being told detailed accounts of thoughts and activities and of being absolutely obeyed in whatever advice he gave. The parish became a cult, centered less on Christ than on the personality and ideas of our priest." In such cases, unless the bishop responds to complaints and replaces the priest with someone better qualified, the only solution is to find another parish.

"Abuse by clergy extends well beyond gross sexual or violent abuse. Guru games are a bad form of abuse," comments Fr. Yves Dubois. "Popular images of the priest as a little God or as an icon of Christ need to be tempered by the Jewish image of the rabbi—a religious specialist, but otherwise just another human being like the rest of us. This of course will affect the whole approach to confession. It needs to be approached with an open mind."

One friend, an adult convert to the Catholic Church who had come from a Protestant background, describes meeting her pastor in his office for her first confession (there were no longer any confessionals in the church). She looks back on the experience with bewilderment, partly because the priest gave her no preparation beforehand and asked no helpful questions once confession had begun:

> *I realize now it should have been a general confession, a review of my life as a whole, but had the idea that only recent sins needed to be mentioned. This meant basically a failure responding to the needs of my aunt and problems in my marriage—sins that were failures of love. But the priest's response was that I was "only human." I had the feeling that I really didn't need to regard my sins as sins. I'm sure he thought he was doing me a favor, but what I needed was a challenge to be more responsible in caring for others, and I needed God's forgiveness.*

At the end of her confession he put his hand on her head but it wasn't clear to her that there was an actual absolution.

A nun with whom I correspond warns of the problem of priests who regard anything that is revealed in confession as a manifestation or consequence of sin in that person's life:

But there are many wounds that are caused by things other than one's own sins and have to be healed in other ways. These may be due to family tragedy, poverty, illness, bereavement, or other people's sins. This is particularly true when people have been abused in childhood or have been victims of war crimes, political or cultural oppression, or other severe abuses. To tell the victims in these situations that their wounds are caused by their own sins and that the remedy is for them to repent and confess only rubs salt in their wounds—yet there are those who do so. In such situations, a priest would do well to refer the person confessing to a qualified therapist, but unfortunately there are priests who regard all therapists as quacks.

Another friend writes:

I don't have any horror stories about confession, just a problem that probably isn't that rare these days—a priest who is an amateur psychologist. He seems embarrassed calling anything a sin. He prefers to say "problem area" and likes to use the phrase "win-win" solutions in the advice he gives. I'm not looking for another confessor but every now and then I remind him that there is a three-letter word for most of the things I tell him in confession.

One correspondent, a convert to the Orthodox Church, described a priest who sometimes hears confessions in his office:

A week before my first confession, my priest had given me a printed sheet that had the prayers of confession and a guide for preparing for confession. It seemed helpful but it in no way prepared me for what happened. During my confession, he had me face a wall in his office decorated not only with icons, which I expected, but family pictures. He began to ask me questions about my relationship to my parents, the kind of childhood I had— sadly, I was sexually abused as a child and my relationship with my parents is still unhealed. I hadn't really anticipated my background being discussed in this way, nor did it help me that I was looking at photos of his own happy family while trying to talk about my own very unhappy family. It was as though these family photos were the baseline evidence of a godly life. I was very confused. I left feeling as though I could never be truly free of whatever it was about me that had this unfortunate childhood. I left feeling not clean but dirty. It was very difficult for me to go to confession the next time, though I did—but the next time in the church rather than his office. Now I am trying to find a way to talk to him about my experience of first confession—to confess my frustrations with it and to see if we can do better the next time.

These stories are meant to be like a yellow light at a traffic crossing. The light's message is not that the road is impassable, but that we must proceed with reasonable care. There are priests to avoid, but the great majority can witness your confession, give helpful advice, and, if needed, assign a healing penance. After one or two confessions with a given priest, it will usually be clear to you whether or not this is a priest to return to, but the chances are he will do. If there are problems, discuss them with him. If it's clear that there is a serious problem, confess to another priest. Only take care that you are not looking for a priest who won't be troubled by your sins or will tell you what you want to hear—that your sins aren't sins at all but excusable choices under the circumstances. Don't forget that the priest listening to your confession sometimes has the responsibility of saying things you may find painful.

"The dream priest I'm looking for to hear my confession," a friend told me, "is so saintly he walks barefoot on water without even noticing his feet are wet—and is deaf as a stone. Until I find him, I'll have to make do with one whose shoes are muddy and who understands only too well what I'm saying."

TRUE CONFESSIONS

And then more would pour out, everything that has been hidden, more and more—sorrow, shame, loneliness, all the old aches, so much released until you overflowed with joy to be rid of it, until it was too late to stop this new joy from taking over your heart.

—AMY TAN, *THE KITCHEN GOD'S WIFE*

A young monk said to the great ascetic Abba Sisoes: "Abba, what should I do? I fell." The elder answered: "Get up!" The monk said: "I got up and I fell again!" The elder replied: "Get up again!" But the young monk asked: "For how long should I get up when I fall?" "Until your death," answered Abba Sisoes.

—SAYINGS OF THE DESERT FATHERS

On Saturday I heard a confession that made me painfully reflect: what is right, what is not? Any principle is shattered by the unique experience of every life. I am but a witness.

—FR. ALEXANDER SCHMEMANN[1]

Sacraments are often called mysteries. This is a way of saying that they are larger and deeper than what we can comprehend or explain. The sacrament of confession is a way of participating in God's incomprehensible mercy. Confession is never our own unaided action. It is God's activity in our lives that inspires the desire to confess those things which damage relationships with God and with others. It is God who enables us to love and makes us regret actions which damage ourselves and others. It is God who gives us faith and makes us regret our betrayals of faith. It is God who draws us toward truth and makes us regret our lies. It is God who illumines the conscience, revealing to us our need for repentance. It is God who gives the courage to confess. Finally, it is God who forgives.

No matter how often it happens, confession is one of life's most intimate events, far more revealing of who we are than taking off all our clothing. It is revealing out loud, to Christ and a witness, the ways we have lost the path that leads into the kingdom of God.

When I started work on this book five years ago, I asked friends to trust me with stories about confession in their own lives, promising that anything they sent me that was included in this book would appear anonymously. Here is a selection from many letters received from lay people, nuns, monks, and priests. I also include several stories or extracts from lectures and articles. Those few which have been published elsewhere or are available on the web are noted.

❖

THE FIRST TIME I HEARD CONFESSION was a couple of weeks after my ordination in 1973, at St. Matthew's Cathedral in Washington, D.C., where John F. Kennedy's requiem Mass was celebrated. The penitent was a tourist who had wandered in almost by accident. "I was on my way to a McDonald's," he said, "but I saw the church and remembered Kennedy's funeral—then I noticed the little green light in the confessional, so I came in. I'm not really sure of what I want."

"Well," I replied, "I hope you don't want a Big Mac with French fries, because if so, you have made a great mistake."

He chuckled, then said: "Look, Father, it's been a long, long time. I'm going to tell you things you have never heard in confession before."

"That's not too difficult," I said. "This is my first confession. Anything you say will be a shock to me." He started to laugh, hard.

I have often heard confessions in very unlikely places, like subways and theaters. The captain of a plane approached me in mid-flight. Terrified, I asked him, "Do you know something that I don't know about this flight?" He assured me that nothing was wrong; he had simply gotten the urge....

[When] confessing even the most dramatic struggles, I have found, people reach for the simplest language, that of a child before a world too confusing to understand. Silent wonder is the most natural response to a revelation that surpasses all words, a beauty that is beyond images; if one must say anything at all, what better way than in a few words that, in their very formalism, protect the infinite majesty of this mystery? The language of the inner life is not the language of experts, nor of eloquent dramatists, nor of a mature and healthy self-acceptance. The language of the inner life is a serene silence, a deep hurt, a boundless desire, and, occasionally, a little laughter.[2]

I FIND THAT THE ACT OF CONFESSION before a priest is just a step in the ongoing cleansing of the soul. I have found that if I confess a certain sin, let's say lying, over the next few days or weeks God will bring to my mind other lies that I have not dealt with, perhaps from years ago. Then I realize I have to deal with those lies also. In other words, the cleansing that happens in confession does not stop when I leave the priest. It continues on—even though sometimes I wish it wouldn't!

IT WAS HELPFUL both to me and to my spiritual father that before my first confession I wrote out for him a spiritual autobiography of myself—when I was baptized, what the sacraments have meant to me over the years, my experiences in various parish and monastic environments, habits of prayer (or lack of such habits!), and anything else that I thought might help him know me better and see what problems needed special attention. Another thing I did was to take the Nicene Creed and write down everything I believed about each phrase of it—that way he could find where my skewed beliefs needed correcting. In the course of writing about the Creed, I discovered that I had some doubts about the Resurrection, mostly thinking that "the age of miracles" was over for us in the age of science.

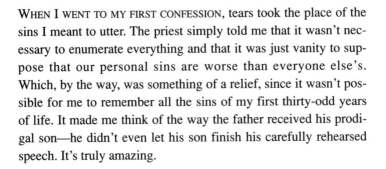

WHEN I WENT TO MY FIRST CONFESSION, tears took the place of the sins I meant to utter. The priest simply told me that it wasn't necessary to enumerate everything and that it was just vanity to suppose that our personal sins are worse than everyone else's. Which, by the way, was something of a relief, since it wasn't possible for me to remember all the sins of my first thirty-odd years of life. It made me think of the way the father received his prodigal son—he didn't even let his son finish his carefully rehearsed speech. It's truly amazing.

A PRIEST OF MY ACQUAINTANCE, a dear friend and very helpful to me for many years, once told me of a confession that changed his life. A man approached him for confession, but was having difficulty getting started. To help him, the priest began the usual questions to see if they might be helpful, but after a few of these, the penitent interrupted him and said, "Listen, Father! I've committed all those sins. I've committed all the sins you've ever heard of, and probably some you haven't. But I'm not here about that. I'm here to confess that I don't tell my wife and kids that I love them."

*A modern confessional in the Franciscan Church of All Nations
at the Garden of Gethsemane, Jerusalem*

I WAS TRAVELING, found a church nearby, and decided to go to confession before the liturgy, if the priest had time. I saw the priest waiting at the front of the church over on the side. I was fully prepared for a long confession. Before I had a chance to say anything, he asked me, "Are you sorry for your sins?" I responded with the utmost sincerity that I was. He said, "In that case, kneel down." A minute later I was on my feet, absolved, receiving a final blessing. This is an extreme solution for an overworked priest, but in fact it was a memorable confession for me.

I REMEMBER AN ELDERLY PRIEST, Fr. John, at the Russian convent in London to which I often went as a layman. He didn't like preaching sermons and he didn't like hearing confessions. He was always extremely laconic. Few words of advice were given. One day, a woman who often came to him for confession told him as usual and at great length the arguments that she had had with her husband. "He said this and I said this and then he said this and I told him he was all wrong and said this and this and this...." In the end, Fr. John simply looked at her and said, "And did it help?" Then he gave her absolution.

Those four words changed her life. She suddenly saw how futile it was to go on arguing all the time, always trying to answer people back, always wanting to have the last word. She suddenly thought, "It doesn't have to be like that at all." She stopped it and changed. It was that very simple word of advice from the priest, put in the form of a question, that made her life different.[3]

ONCE A MAN IN CONFESSION said to Archbishop John Maximovich, who has since been recognized as a saint, "Yes, I see that I have sinned. With my mind, I appreciate that what I've done is wrong, but my heart is like a stone—I feel no sense of sorrow or compunction." His confession was being heard just before the liturgy and there were already many people in the church. Archbishop John said to the man, "Go out into the middle of the church, kneel in front of all these people, and ask their forgiveness, and then come back to me."

The man did so. And when he knelt before the people and asked their forgiveness, a sudden change occurred inside him. Suddenly, the stoniness of his heart was taken away. Suddenly, something that held back his tears of compunction was released, and he was able to weep over his sin, and then he received absolution.[4]

❖

I WAS WORRIED that I might forget what I needed to confess so I made a list of my sins and brought it with me. The priest saw the paper in my hand, took it, looked through the list, tore it up, and gave it back to me. Then he said "Kneel down," and he absolved me. That was my confession even though I never said a word! But I felt truly my sins had been torn up and that I was free of them.

❖

YEARS AGO, when I was in my early twenties and on my own in the big city, I received a call from my mom. It was during Lent and she proceeded to tell me, "Father called and said that you have not been to confession or communion in over three years." When I admitted that this was the case, she gave me the kind of tongue-lashing that only a Russian mother can give, finally making me promise to stop neglecting my faith and find a church in the city.

There was a Greek Orthodox parish nearby. I told the priest the story and asked if I could go to confession. I also asked if he would write a letter to my hometown priest so I would get both him and my mom off my back—such was my attitude in those days! This he agreed to do. He could see I was very nervous. He told me that, from previous experiences, he knew that people sometimes tensed up as soon as they entered the church for confession. If I didn't mind, he said, he would hear my confession right there in the office. He told me that since we were not in church, it was all right to smoke if that made it easier. So I lit up. I was completely relaxed and talked about things I had bottled inside for quite a while. I didn't feel the pressure of time constraints because other people were waiting nor was I worried that I might be talking too loud and other people were hearing what I said. He listened and advised. When I finished, he took me into the church and we stood before the icon of Our Lord and prayed together. Then he prayed for me and gave me penance and absolution. I have never had a more rewarding experience in my life. The next day I went to liturgy and received communion. After the service he gave me the letter I had asked for.

Years later, when I had finally grown up and had gotten rid of my attitude problem and was going to church on a regular basis, I went through a difficult period in my life. I told my parish priest the above story and asked if I could have the same type of confession. He agreed, and once again I was greatly helped.

Since then I've pointed out to friends that, if they're facing a serious problem, they might consider arranging confession at a time when people aren't lined up waiting and that it doesn't have to happen inside the church.

❖

I DON'T SPEAK RUSSIAN REALLY WELL, although I can manage. There was a time when my Russian was even worse than it is now—"kitchen Russian" that I had learned from the parish babushkas pretty well describes it. But because services were in Church Slavonic, the Russian equivalent of Latin, I understood Church Slavonic reasonably well. For years I was better at reading Church Slavonic than Russian. Anyway, it once happened that there was no English-speaking priest available to witness my confession and my Russian was at its worst. But I knew the priest and he knew me. He read the appropriate prayers and asked me to read Psalm 50 in Church Slavonic—"Have mercy on me, O God, in your goodness. In the greatness of your compassion, wipe out my offense...." Then he asked if I recalled the verse. "Lord, do not remember the sins and offenses of my youth." I did recall those words. He asked if I was sorry for all my sins, and I said that I was. With a warm smile and a firm but loving hand on my shoulder, he pronounced the words of restoration. I have to tell you that this was the best confession of my life—yet I offered nothing but the most general of regrets for the "sins and offenses of my youth."

AS AN EPISCOPALIAN, I had never been required to make a private confession. Priests were always available if a member decided to make a confession, but it was optional. In my particular church, private confession was not stressed at all. However, after reading C.S. Lewis's description of his experiences of confession, I began to consider confession seriously.

A few days before Easter Sunday, a visiting priest who had come to my church offered to hear people's confessions. I sensed an inner urge to go to my first confession. To prepare for it, I prayerfully reviewed my whole life. I divided my life into ten-year segments and asked the Lord to bring to my mind sins I had committed during each ten-year period. I wrote everything down.

Many incidents came to my mind from childhood, incidents in which I was not conscious of having sinned but of being sinned against. In considering these incidents I confessed resentment against the adults involved even though I didn't consciously feel resentment. I just wanted to be on the safe side and go ahead and confess in case I were repressing resentment. In addition, plenty of occasions came to my mind in which I knew for sure that I had separated myself from God. I confessed every occasion I could think of when I had sinned.

That first confession was a mountaintop experience. I walked out of the church a different person from the one who walked in. I wasn't really sure I walked out—I may have been floating. Every inner weight was lifted; I felt as light as a feather and utterly and completely cleansed.

A major benefit of confession: Satan is called the accuser, and I am very vulnerable to his accusations. I'm quite receptive to thoughts about how awful I am. But when I confess my sins to a priest and he absolves me on Christ's behalf, it takes this very powerful weapon away from Satan. Confession to a priest frees me not only from real guilt but from the false guilt that comes from Satan. Merely confessing my sins to God in private doesn't have the same effect and doesn't seem to free me from Satan's accusations.

FOR YEARS I FOUND CONFESSION very difficult. This was partly linked to terrible events in my life when I was growing up—sexual abuse within my family. The person who did this has never admitted what he did or sought my forgiveness. A very hard question in my life has been the issue of forgiving someone who has not asked for forgiveness. I cannot say I have yet forgiven him, only that I have learned to pray for him and to pray that he will someday ask to be forgiven and that, when this happens, I will be able to forgive him. In adult life these early experiences have complicated my relations with men and also made it more difficult for me than it might be for other women to confess in the presence of a male, even though he is a priest and someone I trust. Finally I confessed this very problem to my priest. To my surprise, he said that, if it would help, there was a nun he knew who would be willing to hear my confession and that he would be willing to give me absolution following any confessional conversations I had with her. This has been a godsend. I have been doing this for several years now and it has been a great help. At this point in my life, I probably could confess anything and everything to my priest, but the nun has become my spiritual mother.

Years before I was married, I was date-raped by a friend. I'm ashamed to say that for some time after that I had a sexual relationship with the man who did this.

Later in my life, a few years after I had become Orthodox, I was preparing for confession one morning when I felt God bringing those events of years before into my mind and felt I should confess them. I was mortified and didn't understand why they had to be brought up when I had already asked God's forgiveness. I was also upset because the priest was brand new at our church— we hadn't even met face-to-face. His first introduction to me was going to be the knowledge that I had had voluntary sex with a rapist. What an impression that would make! So I prayed and said to God something like, "Can you make me sure You are asking me to do this?" Then I opened my prayer book and the first thing I read was something like this, "My child, if you truly desire healing, you must expose all your sins to the Great Physician." That was enough for me.

In confession, through a torrent of agonized tears, I confessed those sins plus some others. My priest was very kind. After confession he invited me to come and talk to him more if I wanted. He could see that the issue was not resolved.

The journey to healing takes all of one's life. But this particular confession opened to me what has been till now the main part of my healing. Not only did I go to speak with my priest that day but I spoke with him a number of times after that. Memories I had tried to bury began to surface. Finally, I was able to recall and reveal the sexual abuse that had happened to me in childhood and link that with the depression I had been struggling with most of my life. At this point he referred me to a therapist.

This is why I see confession as being so important. When I became honest about my own sins, my healing began to spring forth. I do not think there is healing without confession, no matter what the situation and no matter how much you can point the finger of blame at others. Even regular therapy can be a type of confession and can go a long way in freeing you from disasters in the past. But the best confession is confession in the church.

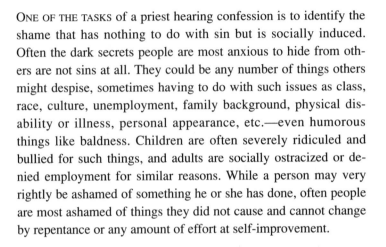

ONE OF THE TASKS of a priest hearing confession is to identify the shame that has nothing to do with sin but is socially induced. Often the dark secrets people are most anxious to hide from others are not sins at all. They could be any number of things others might despise, sometimes having to do with such issues as class, race, culture, unemployment, family background, physical disability or illness, personal appearance, etc.—even humorous things like baldness. Children are often severely ridiculed and bullied for such things, and adults are socially ostracized or denied employment for similar reasons. While a person may very rightly be ashamed of something he or she has done, often people are most ashamed of things they did not cause and cannot change by repentance or any amount of effort at self-improvement.

WE PRIESTS MUST LEARN the specifics and complications of sinful life. We must, to some degree, become psychologists in the sense of becoming doctors of the soul. We must learn that many persons who come to confession come seeking help which we cannot give. And, in those cases, it is up to us to know when confession ends and psychotherapy needs to begin. At first, it may be difficult to tell a parishioner that they need professional help. But when we do, we must be exceptionally careful of the words we use. First, do not deny the power and efficacy of confession and communion. But we need to be prepared to take a critical look at the person before us and decide if their problem is purely spiritual or if it isn't also medical and psychological. We must learn what happens to the personality of drug addicts, alcoholics, habitual liars, and others who are in the grips of forces more powerful than they. It's not necessary for us to become professional psychologists, but a rudimentary knowledge of aberrant personality types is extremely useful to the pastor. And we must be careful not to confuse spiritual advice and guidance with psychological help.[5]

I OFTEN NOTICE, in those who come to confession, a desire to pass painlessly through the operation: either they are content with generalities, or they speak about trifles, keeping silent about the things that ought really to weigh on their conscience. In such cases we have a false shame in facing the priest and, in general, an irresoluteness, such as one feels before every important action, and especially a cowardly fear of having seriously to overturn one's life, full of petty and habitual weaknesses. Real confession, being a beneficial upheaval of the soul, frightens one by its decisive character, by the necessity of changing something, or of simply starting to reflect upon oneself. Here the priest must not be afraid of disturbing this tranquillity and trying to awaken a feeling of genuine repentance.... [The priest must] hear each person's confession as if it were his last confession before death.[6]

AS A PRIEST who hears many confessions, I find the most difficult task is helping penitents overcome a tendency to see themselves as the center of the universe. To the extent God is mentioned, he appears to be a loveless, bureaucratic deity who does nothing but manufacture rules and regulations. The unconfessed but manifest self-centeredness and self-pity are often more shocking than any sin that is confessed. Yet little by little I have the privilege of witnessing conversion happening, usually in slow motion, sometimes in sudden bounds.

THE SACRAMENT OF PENANCE is also a revelation of the Word of God. The priest will insist to his faithful that they must not confuse the spiritual direction they may request of him with the actual forgiveness of sins granted by Christ. It is this forgiveness that is essential. Confession should not become a ritual, a habit or a mere formality. It should be rather an encounter between the repentant sinner and his merciful Savior. It should lead to "a broken and contrite heart" whose brokenness and contrition occur at Jesus' feet.

Apart from the actual confession and absolution, the priest will probably want to offer certain advice and give concrete replies to the questions raised by the penitent. He will say what he feels called to say, briefly and with discretion. He will strive to direct and inform the conscience of the sinner, so that his every thought and action will be increasingly guided by an inner illumination. Above all, the priest will reveal to the penitent that Jesus Christ loves the sinner more than anyone has ever loved him. As much as possible, the priest will avoid speaking with his own words, but will rely upon the words of the Scriptures. The priest will communicate to the penitent the very Word of God, choosing according to the given situation the most appropriate scriptural expressions. In these talks with his priest, the penitent should leave each time with some word from Holy Scripture that speaks directly to his present need.[7]

❖

As A PRIEST, I have found that the most difficult confessions have been those in which I could not absolve someone who had come to me.

I recall one occasion when the person in question clearly rejected the teachings of the Church and had come not because he wished to but under pressure from a relative. I explained to him that sacraments are meaningless if done only under compulsion.

In fact, confession in that particular case, though incomplete, proved to be a step toward real belief, but it was a process that took several years.

The more common experiences are those confessions in which it's obvious that the person has no intention at all of giving up the sin in question. One can be forgiven the same sin again and again but only if a real effort is being made to become free of the activity. If a person confesses adultery but has no intention of ending the adulterous relation, clearly there is no repentance. Repentance—in Greek the word is *metanoia*—means taking a new direction. It's a basic change of heart and mind. If there is no trace of inner conversion, then all I can offer is a readiness to listen and to explain as best I can, but I cannot give absolution.

A less common situation is the person who conceals his sins or is unwilling to recognize that what he is doing is sinful. Again, all I can offer is an explanation as to why a certain action is sinful, perhaps also the suggestion to read a certain book or Bible story or even to see a certain film. I promise the support of my own prayer and give a blessing.

Finally, there are those cases in which the person wants God's forgiveness but not the forgiveness of the person he has sinned against. In these cases, I try to explain that we turn to God *through* others. If I steal something from you, there is no repentance if I want to keep what I stole rather than return it. If I tell you a lie, repentance means telling you the truth. In cases where it is impossible to set things right—a murderer cannot bring back to life the person he killed—he can devote himself to some penitential activity on behalf of those who were victims of his crime or commit himself to some life-preserving or life-saving activity.

When I feel obliged to refuse absolution, I always make clear that this is not a punishment and that our conversation is a step toward absolution. In fact, the next step is often taken before many weeks have passed.

❖

I HAVE THIRTY YEARS OF EXPERIENCE of hearing confessions as a major aspect of my ministry as an Orthodox priest.

I find it difficult to imagine confession except within the context of a long-term friendship between priest and penitent, making it possible for both to be open and frank, and aware of the weaknesses and blind spots of the other. In our parish, we advise a monthly confession, with no pressure but an understanding that less than six confessions a year is likely to lead to difficulties. Parishioners confess to one of the priests in our parish, normally always the same but without hassle if people wish to change. Visitors who come frequently are asked whether they have a spiritual father, and, provided they have one, they are not asked to make a confession in our parish. Whenever possible, it is good if priests can have their bishop as their spiritual father. It builds trust between bishop and priests. Some priests keep their spiritual father other than the bishop if they have had a spiritual father for years before their ordination.

Inevitably, a degree of frustration is to be expected whenever the penitent is aware that the priest is giving advice based on a misunderstanding of what the penitent has confessed. It is a great help if the penitent can feel free to say: "I'm afraid you've got it all wrong."

❖

IN 1990, MY MOTHER DIED UNEXPECTEDLY. I was the one who had to make those terrible decisions involving life-prolonging technology. My world fell apart after her death. My twenty-one-year marriage, unhappy from the start, dissolved within a year, as I demanded solitude in which to heal and look honestly at my life for the first time. In my anger and confusion, I fled from the narrow notions of God—and of Orthodoxy—which had held my world together for many years. A profound emptiness took their place. I couldn't stand the thought of entering a church or saying a prayer. I felt as if I had been wrenched from a normal existence by a whirlwind and set down alone in a desert.

I began to pursue pleasure recklessly; it was a fleeting antidote for the despair I felt when alone. I became relentlessly hedonistic, and no command of God or man could stop me from obtaining the comfort I craved. This soon brought its own anguish, and though the whirlwind had seemingly swept God out of my heart, images of penitents from the Bible kept invading my thoughts—the Prodigal, the Samaritan woman, Mary Magdalene.

One day, I found myself sitting on the bathroom floor, crying and holding a bottle of aspirin and wondering how many it would take to do myself in. As soon as the question formed, I knew that for my children's sake I could never kill myself. And it was at that moment that a very small voice within me called my name. It was barely a whisper, but over the next days and weeks I found myself listening more and more attentively for that compelling voice, finally focusing on it most of the time. To my astonishment I discovered that a much greater God than I had conceived of before, a God who couldn't be described or named or quantified, was seeking me—and He had never stopped seeking me!

Coming back to God was finally coming to sanity, a slow awakening from nightmare. I began to tame my wild behavior. The grief I had felt became a sorrow for what I had done to myself and my family, and a longing to bind myself to what was good and true. It happened that months before, I had rented an apartment across the street from a Greek Orthodox church. It was a parish with which I had no affiliation; I didn't know the priest. With trepidation, I called him one day and made an appointment for confession. It had been over two years since I had entered an Orthodox church.

That warm afternoon, just two weeks before Pascha, I knelt and blurted it all out. As the priest placed the stole over my head, a great feeling of relief—it was over!—and of joyful gratitude enveloped me. Spiritually I will always be kneeling there, aware of my plentiful weaknesses and of the mortal (or rather immortal) danger of ever walking away again.

Confession is a spring in that desert I always seem to be creating for myself, a source of living water, and I return again and again for refreshment. Though my life now is happier than I could ever have imagined, that happiness is undercut by a continual sorrow at my refractory nature. God in His mercy has shown me the way of repentance.

ONE NIGHT, VERY LATE, God called back this particular prodigal son. I phoned a priest I knew right away and asked to make my confession. He said to come over first thing in the morning, which I did. Now I'm a monk. What would have happened if that priest hadn't answered the phone, or put me off until it was convenient for him? I don't know; God knows. And I am everlastingly grateful to God for His mercy, and for the kindness of His servants, good and faithful priests.

ONE OF THE MOST IMPORTANT CONFESSIONS I ever made was during a time when I was wrestling with the claim of the Church to be the only path to salvation. At the time I was thinking a great deal about the horror of anti-Semitism and other kinds of ethnic hatred —ethnic arrogance and triumphalism, which you sometimes hear expressed in the Church. The subject was very real to me. I had an image in my mind of the Jews being taken to their deaths in a camp like Auschwitz. The train pulls up, the Jews are unloaded, the selection is made, and the condemned are led away to the furnaces, where they are gassed and cremated. Their spirits rise to heaven, where they find themselves in yet another train pulling into another camp. There's another selection. The Jews are condemned and led away once again—to eternal destruction. This was the only sense I could make out of the claim that there is no salvation outside the Church. I found it more and more difficult to be a Christian, imagining that such poor, innocent people were being condemned over and over again. I could not feel good about my own salvation at their expense.

So I took this to confession. The priest, a Dutchman, had been a teenager in Holland during the war. His family had given refuge to Jews during the war, but the Jews were discovered and taken to Auschwitz, and they never came back. His mother had been arrested but luckily later released. I told him my problem. His answer was very interesting. All he said was, "If you love the Jews, you will be the best Christian you can be. Remember the story of the Rich Young Man? Maybe that's something for you."

It was like a riddle, or an itch on the back in a spot you cannot quite reach. He didn't tell me why he mentioned the rich young man or what the story might have to do with my problem. I thought about the story, about Jesus saying, "If you would be perfect, sell all you have, give it to the poor, and follow me." I realized the priest wasn't suggesting that I actually sell all I have. He was saying, you must be unconditionally committed to following Christ. You must throw yourself into it heart and soul. Don't hold anything back. Don't try to imagine where you stand in relation to other people. "Sell all you have"—stand before Christ, with nothing to tie you to anything else.

This was enormously helpful to me, especially in the face of growing relativism in a society where it's considered a gross injustice to embrace anything that you claim is ultimate truth. This is the post-modern dilemma. Because how can you live without ultimate truth? How can you live with some kind of wishy-washy principle that is "true for you"?

❖

LAST SUNDAY I GOT INTO A TERRIBLE FIGHT on my way to church. It was over a parking place. I had driven around for over half an hour trying to find parking and was getting more and more frustrated. Finally I start to park and this car screams up behind me. The driver lays on the horn and turns his bright lights on and off. I have no idea what's happening. The guy pulls up beside me and starts cursing me for going so slow. I explain that I'm parking and he tells me to . . . I'd better leave out what he said. I say the same thing back. Before you know it, we're screaming obscenities at each other and I am ready to just get out of the car and go at it. I hear myself think "let this go" and "don't get into this" but I can't stop. I open the door and the guy pulls away.

Just then I hear the church bells and I run into church. Once inside, I try to pray for forgiveness, but I am so furious I'm shaking. I realize I'm in no state to receive communion. I feel terrible about my actions. My mouth feels like an outhouse for all the filth I've been screaming. I am such a hypocrite.

I remember that my godmother is downstairs, making preparations for lunch after the service, so I go downstairs and tell her what happened. She suggests I send a note to Fr. _____ explaining what happened and asking forgiveness and a blessing to take communion. I run upstairs with my note and wait. During the service he sends a note back saying that God forgives but that I have to forgive the man whose day I ruined also. I feel so bad about it all. Even though I know God forgives and I've been given a blessing to receive communion, it's all been just terrible—the fight and my temper and lack of control, the drama at church, everything. As I go up for Father's blessing and to kiss the cross at the end of liturgy, he says, "Don't be distracted by Satan."

❖

AFTER VESPERS, folks begin to leave the church. I move to the right of the sanctuary and find a place to sit next to the wall near the front. The service has ended but the candles remain lit and there is a pensive quiet that seems to make the silence louder and the space a bit larger. You can hear shoes squeak on the wooden floor as people move across the sanctuary to the door or join the line waiting to make confession.

In the corner to the right of the iconostasis, the cross and Gospel seem to wait for me to approach. I'm not very comfortable with this yet. Making confession is new to me and I never know what to say. I usually sit in a chair by the wall and everyone seems to wait either sitting or standing in a loose line strung be-

hind each other toward the vestibule. Usually there are not many
people who wait to confess on a normal Saturday night. There are
probably not more than four or five except during Lent. The line
lengthens as Pascha approaches.

I must admit there is a feeling of companionship somehow,
even as we sit separately in the darkened chapel. There is not a lot
of contact or talk as we wait. And when glances do meet on occasion, usually the slight smile of acknowledgment fades as your
eyes fall to the floor. I sit in my chair, hands folded nervously on
my lap. There was only one time I just couldn't face the process
and left. It had been raining and as I sat waiting I tried to talk myself out of staying because if I missed my bus, I'd miss my sub-
way train, and on and on, until I got up and walked out the door.
But as I walked in the rain to the corner I realized that it wasn't
the commute I dreaded but confession.

I have problems with trying to know what to say. It's not that I
don't recognize that I'm a sinner, but I seem to accept sin as part of
human nature or personality, which makes it something that is not
going to really change very much or go away. Thinking like this
kind of normalizes relations with sin while at the same time ignor-
ing the darkest consequences or source of sin. It's like favored nation trading status with a dictatorship. We want all the benefits of
trade but overlook the violations of human rights and integrity.

There are a lot of problems with this, I realize, but in some
ways I've used sin to define myself and not necessarily in a nega-
tive light. I've noticed that when my old friends and I get together
and talk we spend hours laughing and retelling stories about our
wild youth. It seems, however, that those stories are in many ways
stories about how much we enjoyed committing sins. Maybe that's
where the expression "sins of youth" comes from. Sin is expected
in the young. Of course we're not talking about major crimes
against people, but when I stop to think about it, they may be
crimes against God and certainly the teachings of the Church.

I still have a tendency to see the wild side as freer than the
temperate, and to see rebellion as much more positive than nega-

tive and a way to distance oneself from the banality and medioc-
rity of mass society.

My impatience and temper, my sarcasm, my so-called "biting
wit" are ways I define "me as me" in the world. Of course, those
somehow become translated and calculated in a vast personal al-
gebra of character and predisposition.

Unfortunately, I have a tendency to reduce those traits into a
continuum of understandable explanations and excuses for my
personal behavior and relations to others and the world. I weave
stories and reasons into a systematic construction that leads me to
conclude that what I have done is generally acceptable given the
circumstances of my life. I reduce my sins to a group of personality traits.

As I sit waiting for our priest to complete hearing the confession of the person before me, I consider what I will say. I think
about my actions during the period since my last confession and
sort out what a sin is from what it is not. It's not hard to recall my
anger or sharp words. It's not hard to recall my foul mouth and
quick temper. It's not hard to recall a few too many vodkas. I
count and measure, divide by time and guilt, and usually come up
with a list of behaviors that I'm not proud of. I guess being
ashamed about something is a pretty good sign that some definition or variable of sin may be involved. A guilty conscience was
the first compass I had in learning how to recognize sin.

Though I don't like doing it, and I don't do it well, there is a
great respect and intimacy in the act of making confession and
that seems understood and respected by everyone in the church.
There is a quietness in waiting that surrounds us in our quandary
and distress.

❖

CONFESSION IS A WAY to bring your sins out into the open. It's not
that anything can be hidden from God, but without naming the sin
it seems to remain part of the ordinary. Without naming the sin it

camouflages itself and nestles into the dark brush of our normal behavior. Once I heard the weeping and crying, I realized that it was the soul in labor. More a casting off, however, than a birth, though the pain is the same. Struggling to push and haul and break the stones which seal the soul from God. The act of confession is a ritual of naming aloud the hidden secrets of our own conscience which distance us from its Divine Source. We realize we are trapped in a prison of our own design. At first I would try and give a vignette of the circumstances and reasons why I had sinned. I'd try to explain my anger, to justify my behavior. But my priest would stop me and suggest that I not make excuses—just acknowledge the sin, name it for what it is. I didn't need to say why I was angry at my wife and or made a hurtful comment. I had to take responsibility before God for doing it and ask forgiveness.

❖

CONFESSION SEEMS TO UNCOVER the dark sadnesses in the heart and mind and, though no revelation to God, creates a sense of freedom from carrying the terrible concerns which weigh us down in life. And it is my own sins that are the burden. I have loaded too much baggage on my back. I am carrying around a weight that I have created and placed there and, as the dead stones I struggle with increase, my breath shortens and I gasp for air. The more I sin, the heavier the burden and the journey seem to become. Often that sense of impossibility actually leads to more sin. We are a very clever and devious bunch of creatures because we hide the heaviest stones from ourselves and wonder at the difficulty we have in traversing the vast landscape of our lives.

❖

I AM A VERY STRONG-MINDED PERSON, as is my priest. At times we disagree with each other's opinions on politics and social issues and I feel the need to stand up for what I believe. Once, I was having a particularly strong disagreement with him. I was trying hard to convince him of the reasonableness of my opinion and to show that my position had a theological foundation.

All the time I was trying to argue my position, I was aware of areas of sin in my life which required confession. I thought, "How can I confess to this priest? How will he respect my thinking if I expose to him my weaknesses and sinfulness? Won't that undermine my argument? He'll just have more reasons to disregard what I say and think."

Finally I realized that this way of thinking just provided ground for more sins of pride and ego. I had to be willing to be humbled. I also had to realize that we are all sinners and that this doesn't negate the better thoughts and inclinations that God inspires in us. It's possible to be used by God—to have something important to say—and still be a very weak vessel. Also, I had to separate out my relationship to the pastor as a fellow Christian from my relationship to him as priest, representing Christ in the sacraments. I needed to confess to God, and be absolved by God, regardless of the human relationship. I resolved to confess to this priest, to submit my life more fully to Christ and to the pursuit of holiness, and to humbly seek God's wisdom in my own thinking. If my opinions and beliefs about life and the world we live in are to have any weight of moral truth, it will only be through my willingness to be humble and to bow before the Lord regularly in the sacrament of confession.

❖

I WORK IN THE CLOTHING SECTION of a department store. Many times I've stolen things that caught my eye—a scarf one week, a sweater the next. I had a kind of self-imposed rule to limit myself to one "gift" per week. I had various ways of justifying this in my mind. I know I'm not the only one who does it where I work and I tried to think of it as something "everyone does." I also argued to myself that it was compensation for being underpaid, except that, to be honest the pay is fair, and even if it weren't, stealing is stealing. I didn't even steal things I really needed and I never enjoyed wearing them as I would enjoy something I had paid for. Anything stolen felt soiled—it never was really mine.

It was not easy to bring this to confession. The idea of telling our priest that I was a thief was horrible even to think about. So embarrassing! But finally I did, though with a little help. He could see there was something I was holding back and reminded me that it wasn't him I was confessing to, it was Christ, and that he had also done many things he was ashamed of. He was only a witness to my confession. Somehow this uncorked the bottle.

I HAVE DEALT WITH BEING FAT all my life. I have struggled with my weight since childhood and am familiar with the patterns of both eating and dieting. During the diet there is a point where people give in. They just let the desire for the food before them become more important than all the reasons for dieting. The problem that consistently surfaces for me is that after eating that piece of cheesecake I don't stop. In fact, once I have broken the diet in one single act, the most important part of success is stopping there. No one gets fat by eating one piece of cheesecake, but in that one "fall" from the diet an excuse is created which justifies eating more. What do I say when I step over any line I have set for myself in regard to a particular unwanted behavior limit? "What the hell." I'm not just talking about saying okay to a piece of cheesecake. How many times have I used that expression as the beginning of a carefree approach to sin? I can recount a litany of self-destructive and sinful behaviors that usually begin with the words, "What the hell." These are the three heaviest words I know—and I'm still having to carry them to confession.

BY FAR MY HARDEST CONFESSION was to admit that I was a murderer. I killed at least three people when I was a soldier in Vietnam. As I saw it at the time, it was them or me. But in the years since then I have never stopped thinking about what happened. I was in therapy for a while and it did me some good, but I continued to feel haunted by those whom I had killed. Finally, partly thanks to advice from my wife, I brought it to confession. This was the first time I ever called what I had done "murder." I thought my priest might tell me not to use this word, because I was only doing what was required of me as a soldier, but he just asked me what had happened and I just told him. I started to cry and he also cried. It was a long confession. Before giving me absolution, he asked if I would try to find a way to help the war's survivors. I did some research and eventually got involved in a project to help people who had been injured in the war—mainly amputees. I've now gone back to Vietnam several times.

❖

I REMEMBER AN OLD WOMAN who came and said to me [in confession] that she did not know how to live. She would spend whole nights seeing in her dreams and in her memories all the evil she had done. She went to the doctor, who gave her pills, and it was only worse because her memories became hallucinations. What could she do? I said to her, "Remember, God grants us not only once to live through our life but to live and relive our lives time and again until all the evil of it is expurgated. When evil stands up from the past before you, ask yourself: Now, with the experience of life I have acquired, now, would I be the person I was then? Would I say these murderous words, would I do such and such action which was evil? And if you can say sincerely, 'Oh no, with what I have learned from life, now, placed in the same situation, I would never, never do the same'—then you can say, 'Lord, forgive me this particular moment of my past,' and know that you are free. If you can say that with all your heart, with all sincerity, with all the truth there is in you, then it will not come back to you."[8]

ONE OF THE MOST DIFFICULT PROBLEMS I have encountered in hearing confessions concerned a woman whose only son had died in
an automobile accident. She is a devout believer, a very faithful
person, well educated, but her son's death made her furious with
God, whom she held responsible for her son's death. God had allowed this tragedy to happen and she felt as if God had committed a sin, an unforgivable sin. For a long time she had to struggle
every single day with her grief and anger. She sometimes came to
me in confession. There was very little I could say. I knew it
would do her no good to remind her of the Resurrection. All I
could do was suggest that she regularly stand or kneel before the
icon of the Mother of God holding her Divine Son. I said to her,
"The Mother of God knows how you feel. She also lost her son.
She had to watch the most innocent man who ever lived die before her eyes. Ask her to cry with you. Ask her to help you forgive God." She did as I asked, but it was a long and hard struggle.
For three years she felt unable to receive communion. "How can I
receive communion," she said to me, "if I am angry with the God
whom I would receive?" Finally the day came. She told me that
morning, "I am ready for communion. God has helped me to forgive God." I know she still suffers from her son's death, but she
has been given a deeper communion with God.

ONE OF MY BEST CONFESSIONS followed reading a couple of
Walker Percy novels. Time and again Percy described the problem of "everydayness." Some of his characters are backing into
suicidal despair through sheer boredom. They tend to be most
alive when their lives are endangered. As Percy puts it in an
essay, "Man, of all creatures, is capable of feeling good during
hurricanes and sad on ordinary Wednesday afternoons."[9] I realized that a big problem in my own life was being trapped in a
state of everydayness and this was what I confessed the next time

I had a chance. I wondered if my priest would understand what I was talking about—the sin of everydayness!—but I didn't have to say much to define what I meant. He said, "That's my struggle too." When I look back, I realize that confession was a turning point in my life.

❖

OUR CHURCH WAS CROWDED during the Pascha service, with all of the regular parishioners and many visitors and guests. I had had a wonderful Lent and was very aware of both my sinfulness and God's great mercies and redemption, and I was enjoying the blessing of singing out, "Christ is risen from the dead, trampling down death by death, and upon those in the tombs bestowing life!" Things were going fine in the service until our priest's sermon. He made a statement that was not meant to be offensive, but someone in the congregation took issue with it. At that point, this man blurted out his disagreement and engaged in a "discussion" with the priest over the words he'd used in the sermon. The priest was clearly upset by this interruption and its inappropriateness. He continued the sermon, raising his voice and turning red with anger. After a few sentences, he asked for us to wait a few minutes, turned to the altar and prayed. When he returned to the sermon, he was much calmer and clearly at peace. At the end, he went up to the man who had interrupted the sermon and embraced him.

I thought that everything was resolved and we would finish the liturgy with no more thought of it, but when the priest began the eucharistic prayers, he beckoned for a visiting priest to come to the altar with him. They stood there together near the altar as the first priest made his confession to the second.

I was so moved by this very visible portrayal of the Paschal mystery! In the course of the liturgy, we had seen sin, repentance, and reconciliation, both between two humans and between God and man. The final act of confession showed that reconciliation is possible only through Christ's great sacrifice for us and His victory over death and sin. Truly, Christ has risen from the dead,

trampling down death by death, and upon those in the tomb bestowing life!

AS A PRIEST serving at a university, one thing I have found again
and again, so consistently that it is something I have come to expect, is that when I hear confessions, I find I am listening to and
witnessing people at their best, an ironic twist, on the surface of it,
but not when you reflect on it: people are coming to make a turn
back to God. This is when we are at our best, our hearts softened,
our souls humbled, our wills disposed to show mercy to others.

FR. ALEXANDER SCHMEMANN was my confessor at Seminary. He
frequently asked if I remembered that God loves me. This is a
simple thing that in fact we sort of take for granted and then it's
almost like forgetting it. And of course if we really knew God
loved us, we would never have to be afraid of anything. I frequently ask my parishioners, especially children and young people, if they know that God loves them, and tell them to always try
to keep it in mind. Children love to hear it.

I ONCE CONFESSED before a priest who was attached to our parish
and I felt as if I were shining with light afterward. I was also surprised that he exchanged the Paschal kiss—the kiss of peace—
with me after confession. I talked with him about my surprise and
also the profound relief and joy I experienced. He said that Fr.
Alexander Schmemann had been his spiritual father and had
taught him that joy is the aim of confession.

A SERMON ON CONFESSION

Many come to confession and repeat only things which they have read in manuals of devotion or which other people have told them about. I would like to start where I start with a child and attract your attention to the fact that our situation is the same.

When a child comes to confession, usually he brings either on paper or by memory a long list, or a short list, of sins. And when he has finished, I always say, "Are these things which break your heart? Are these things which you feel are wrong in you? Did you invent for yourself this confession?" And most of the time the answer is, "No, my mother gave me this list because that makes her cross!" After that I usually have a conversation with the mother. But as far as the child is concerned, it has nothing to do with him, it is not *his* confession. It is the judgment which the parents have established, accusations against him.

The same could be asked about grown-up people who come with lists of sins which they have found in manuals, or been told by others to consider.

And the answer is always the same: it is not my confession, yet it is a challenge which I was given.

And then, the next move, indeed, is to ask, "What do you know of Christ? Does he attract you? Do you like him? Does he mean anything to you?" And the answer is varied. Some say, "No, I know him from afar off, I know him from the Church, from what I was taught, but I never had a personal attitude to him." Then the answer is, "Find out. Read the Gospel and try to find out what Christ is like."

And the next move: Ask yourself, "Do I like Him? Would I wish to be his disciple, his friend?" If the answer is "no," then begin to think about your whole situation, because if Christ means nothing, if you dislike him, if he is no image of what *you* would like to be, then you must start a long, long way away.

But if you can say, "Yes! I like him, I can respect him, I can admire him. Yes, I would like to be his personal friend if he was here," then my next question will be, "Do you know what friendship is?"

Friendship consists most of all in choosing someone among all the people to be to you the one you treasure above all, whom you admire, by whom you are prepared to stand in case of danger or unpleasantness; one to whom you wish to give joy.

Ask yourself in what way you have tried in the past week to give some joy to the Lord Jesus Christ, or in what way have you been for him a cause of pain.

Begin to re-examine your status as a Christian. If you can say, yes, I choose him as a friend, begin to ask yourself every day, *every day*: What have I done, said, thought, felt, been, which can be to him a joy or a pain?

And when you will come to confession *that is* what you must bring. Between the last confession and today's confession this is what I have been: an unfaithful friend, an indifferent friend, a cowardly friend. . . .

Think in those terms and your confession will be your own— the truth, the rock bottom of your life and heart, the truth about your relationship with Christ.

We confess to him, we open our hearts to him. We tell him all that separates us from him—not lists of formal sins but what we feel in our hearts is our unfaithfulness; what we feel in our hearts separates us, because in spite of the words of love and of veneration which we sometimes pronounce, we act in a way that nails him to the cross again.

— Metropolitan Anthony Bloom, extracted from a sermon given at All Saints Russian Orthodox Cathedral in London in September 1999

PSALMS TO READ
IN PREPARING FOR CONFESSION
(Selections)

Psalm 32:

Blessed is he whose transgression is forgiven,
    whose sin is covered.
Blessed is the man to whom the LORD imputes no iniquity,
    and in whose spirit there is no deceit.

When I declared not my sin, my body wasted away
    through my groaning all day long.
For day and night your hand was heavy upon me;
    my strength was dried up as by the heat of summer.

I acknowledged my sin to you,
    and I did not hide my iniquity;
I said, "I will confess my transgressions to the LORD";
    then you forgave the guilt of my sin....

Psalm 38:

O LORD, rebuke me not in your anger,
    nor chasten me in your wrath!
For your arrows have sunk into me,
    and your hand has come down on me.

There is no soundness in my flesh
    because of your indignation;
there is no health in my bones
    because of my sin.
For my iniquities have gone over my head;
    they weigh like a burden too heavy for me.

My wounds grow foul and fester
    because of my foolishness,
I am utterly bowed down and prostrate;
    all the day I go about mourning.
For my loins are filled with burning,
    and there is no soundness in my flesh.
I am utterly spent and crushed;
    I groan because of the tumult of my heart. . . .

Do not forsake me, O LORD!
    O my God, be not far from me!
Make haste to help me,
    O Lord, my salvation!

Psalm 51:

Have mercy on me, O God,
    according to your steadfast love;
    according to your abundant mercy blot out my transgressions.
Wash me thoroughly from my iniquity,
    and cleanse me from my sin!

For I know my transgressions,
    and my sin is ever before me.
Against you, you only, have I sinned,
    and done that which is evil in your sight,
so that you are justified in your sentence
    and blameless in your judgment.

Behold, I was brought forth in iniquity,
    and in sin did my mother conceive me.

Behold, you desire truth in the inward being;
    therefore teach me wisdom in my secret heart.
Purge me with hyssop, and I shall be clean;
    wash me, and I shall be whiter than snow.
Fill me with joy and gladness;
    let the bones which you have broken rejoice.
Hide your face from my sins,
    and blot out all my iniquities.

Create in me a clean heart, O God,
    and put a new and right spirit within me.
Cast me not away from your presence,
    and take not your holy Spirit from me.
Restore to me the joy of your salvation,
    and uphold me with a willing spirit.

Then I will teach transgressors your ways,
    and sinners will return to you.
Deliver me from blood-guiltiness, O God,
    you God of my salvation,
    and my tongue will sing aloud of your deliverance.

O Lord, open my lips,
    and my mouth shall show forth your praise.
For you take no delight in sacrifice;
    were I to give a burnt offering, you would not be pleased.
The sacrifice acceptable to God is a broken spirit;
    a broken and contrite heart, O God, you will not despise.

Do good to Zion in your good pleasure;
    rebuild the walls of Jerusalem,
then you will delight in right sacrifices,
    in burnt offerings and whole burnt offerings;
    then bulls will be offered on your altar.

Psalm 102:

Hear my prayer, O Lord;
   let my cry come to you!
Do not hide your face from me
   in the day of my distress!
Incline your ear to me;
   answer me speedily in the day when I call!

For my days pass away like smoke,
   and my bones burn like a furnace.
My heart is smitten like grass, and withered;
   I forget to eat my bread.
Because of my loud groaning
   my bones cleave to my flesh.
I am like a vulture of the wilderness,
   like an owl of the waste places;
I lie awake,
   I am like a lonely bird on the housetop.
All the day my enemies taunt me,
   those who deride me use my name for a curse.
For I eat ashes like bread,
   and mingle tears with my drink,
because of your indignation and anger;
   for you have taken me up and thrown me away.
My days are like an evening shadow;
   I wither away like grass.
But you, O Lord, are enthroned for ever;
   your name endures to all generations.
You will arise and have pity on Zion;
    it is the time to favor her;
    the appointed time has come.
For your servants hold her stones dear,
   and have pity on her dust.
The nations will fear the name of the LORD,
   and all the kings of the earth your glory.

For the LORD will build up Zion,
    he will appear in his glory;
he will regard the prayer of the destitute,
    and will not despise their supplication. . . .

Psalm 130:

Out of the depths I cry to you, O Lord!
    Lord, hear my voice!
Let your ears be attentive
    to the voice of my supplications!

If you, O LORD, should mark iniquities,
    Lord, who could stand?
But there is forgiveness with you,
    that you may be feared.

I wait for the Lord, my soul waits,
    and in his word I hope;
my soul waits for the Lord
    more than watchmen for the morning,
    more than watchmen for the morning.

O Israel, hope in the LORD!
    For with the LORD there is steadfast love,
    and with him is plenteous redemption.
The Lord will redeem Israel
    from all his iniquities.

Psalms for after Confession

Psalm 23:

The Lord is my shepherd, I shall not want;
    he makes me lie down in green pastures.
He leads me beside still waters;
    he restores my soul.
He leads me in paths of righteousness
    for his name's sake.

Even though I walk through the valley of the shadow of death,
    I fear no evil,
for you are with me;
    your rod and your staff
    they comfort me.

You prepare a table before me
    in the presence of my enemies;
you anoint my head with oil,
    my cup overflows.
Surely goodness and mercy shall follow me
    all the days of my life
and I shall dwell in the house of the LORD
    for ever.

Psalm 103:

Bless the LORD, O my soul,
    and all that is within me, bless his holy name!
Bless the LORD, O my soul,
    and forget not all his benefits,
who forgives all your iniquity,
    who heals all your diseases,
who redeems your life from the Pit,
    who crowns you with steadfast love and mercy,
who satisfies you with good as long as you live
    so that your youth is renewed like the eagle's.

The LORD works vindication
    and justice for all who are oppressed.
He made known his ways to Moses,
    his acts to the people of Israel.
The LORD is merciful and gracious,
    slow to anger and abounding in steadfast love.
He will not always chide,
    nor will he keep his anger for ever.
He does not deal with us according to our sins,
    nor requite us according to our iniquities.
For as the heavens are high above the earth,
    so great is his steadfast love toward those who fear him;
as far as the east is from the west,
    so far does he remove our transgressions from us.
As a father pities his children,
    so the LORD pities those who fear him.
For he knows our frame;
    he remembers that we are dust.

As for man, his days are like grass;
    he flourishes like a flower of the field;
for the wind passes over it, and it is gone,
    and its place knows it no more.

But the steadfast love of the LORD is from everlasting to
    everlasting
  upon those who fear him,
  and his righteousness to children's children,
to those who keep his covenant
  and remember to do his commandments.
The LORD has established his throne in the heavens,
  and his kingdom rules over all.
Bless the LORD, O you his angels,
  you mighty ones who do his word,
  hearkening to the voice of his word!
Bless the LORD, all his hosts,
  his ministers that do his will!
Bless the LORD, all his works,
  in all places of his dominion.
Bless the LORD, O my soul!

NOTES

A Three-Letter Word

1. Fr. Alexander Schmemann, *St. Vladimir's Seminary Quarterly*, vol. 5, no. 3 (Fall 1961): 38-44; also posted on the web— <www.schmemann.org/byhim/reflectionsonconfession.html>.

2. "Garrison Keillor and the Hopeful Gospel Quartet"; Sony Music, Epic label, EK52901.

3. Fr. Alexander Schmemann, *St. Vladimir's Seminary Quarterly*.

4. For the full text, see pages 110-20 of the Farrar Straus & Giroux edition of Walker Percy's *Love in the Ruins* published in 1971.

5. Bishop Kallistos Ware, in a talk "Approaching Christ the Physician: The True Meaning of Confession and Anointing" at an Orthodox Peace Fellowship retreat in Vézelay, France, in April 1999; the full text is posted at <www.incommunion.org/kal3.htm> on the web.

6. Garrison Keillor, *News from Lake Wobegon*, "Letter from Jim," on the first of four compact discs, a Prairie Home Companion recording, 1983, PHC 15377.

7. "On the Duty of Civil Disobedience."

8. Fr. Alexander Schmemann, *St. Vladimir's Seminary Quarterly*.

Foundations

1. Dorothy Day, *The Long Loneliness* (New York: Harper, 1952), 9-10.

2. "We Confess Our Sins," by Fr. Thomas Hopko (Syosset, N.Y.: Orthodox Church in America, 1993).

A Short History of Confession

1. Now at the Royal Museum for Fine Arts in Antwerp, Belgium, it originally was painted for the bishop's chapel in Tournai.

2. One of the small differences that have evolved within the Orthodox Church is the text used by the priest at the end of confession. In the Greek tradition, "My spiritual child, who has confessed to my humble person: I, humble and a sinner, have no power on earth to forgive sins. Only God does this. Through the divine voice of our Lord Jesus Christ who, after the resurrection, said to the Apostles: 'If you forgive the sins of anyone, they are forgiven; if you retain them, they are retained,' I am given the courage to say: Whatsoever you have said to my humble person, or whatever you have failed to say whether through ignorance, forgetfulness or whatever reason, may God forgive you in this present age and the age to come." In the Russian tradition, the priest says: "May our Lord and God, Jesus Christ, by the grace and compassion of his love for man, pardon all your faults, child _____, and I, the unworthy priest _____, by his authority given me, pardon and absolve you of all your sins: in the name of the Father and of the Son and of the Holy Spirit."

3. James Dallen, *The Reconciling Community: The Rite of Penance* (Collegeville, Minnesota: The Liturgical Press, 1991), 33. Later in his life, distressed at the Church's readiness to pardon those who had abandoned the Church in periods of persecution, Tertullian would argue that there were sins which the Church was not permitted to forgive after baptism. He sided with the Montanists, a sect renowned for the asceticism of its adherents and their readiness to embrace martyrdom.

4. Homilies on Leviticus, 24.

5. Dallen, *The Reconciling Community,* 48-49.

6. Fr. Alexander Schmemann, *St. Vladimir's Seminary Quarterly.*

7. Letters 134, 4; Gary Wills, *St. Augustine* (London and New York: Penguin Books, 2000), 110.

8. Dallen, *The Reconciling Community,* 92.

9. Translation by Thomas Merton in *Wisdom of the Desert* (New York: New Directions, 1960), 27, 29.

10. Bishop Kallistos Ware, "Approaching Christ the Physician."

11. Dallen, *The Reconciling Community,* 131.

12. Ibid., 112.

13. Ibid., 114.

14. Ibid., 115-16.

15. Ibid., 117.

16. Ibid., 150.

17. Ibid., 161.

18. For an evenhanded treatment of the Great Schism, see *The Orthodox Church,* revised edition, by Timothy Ware (London and New York: Penguin Books, 1993), 43-62.

19. Originally indulgences had been a remission by the Church of severe penalties imposed for grave sins in the era of canonical penance. By Luther's time, however, the word referred to a doctrinal system that had been developed by scholastic theologians when disputes arose among them on the relation between contrition and absolution and the exercise of "the power of the keys," the phrase referring to Christ having said to Peter, "I give to you the keys to the kingdom of heaven. What you bind on earth shall be bound in heaven; what you loose on earth shall be loosed in heaven" (Mt 16:19). A theological consensus eventually emerged that, while the sacrament of penance removed the debt of eternal punishment, there was yet a "temporal" punishment for sin which the Church could remit through indulgences. Indulgences came to mean a shortening of time spent after death in purgatory on the way to heaven.

20. A famous Russian priest of the late nineteenth century, St. John of Kronstadt, used to have people shout out their sins just before communion during the liturgy. He would then do a prayer of absolution over the thousands of people attending in order to help in preparing them to receive communion. He did this because he could no longer deal with the thousands of people who wanted to come to him for confession.

21. Letter to the author.

Basic Stories

1. For a fuller meditation on the parable of the Prodigal Son, see Henri Nouwen's *The Return of the Prodigal Son: Meditations on Fathers, Brothers, and Sons* (New York: Doubleday, 1992).

2. *The Sacrament of Penance* (Oxford: St. Stephen's Press, 2001), 11-24.

3. The Book of Enoch is an apocalyptic text that has survived in the Ethiopian biblical canon. The complete Book of Daniel, including the

hymn of praise sung by the young men in the furnace, is found only in Catholic and Orthodox editions of the Bible, or in Protestant editions that include the "apocryphal" books.

4. *Butler's Lives of the Saints*, ed. Herbert Thurston, S.J., and Donald Attwater (New York: Kenedy & Sons, 1963), III: 609.

Standing at the Four Crossroads

1. In Orthodox Christianity, the Creed is referred to as the "symbol of faith." The Greek word "symbol" means "that which brings together."

2. "Letter to N. D. Fonvizina," *Selected Letters of Fyodor Dostoyevsky*, trans. Andrew MacAndrew, ed. Joseph Frank and David Goldstein (New Brunswick, N.J.: Rutgers University Press, 1987), 68. One finds a similar passage in a notebook entry written in 1881, the year he died: "I believe in Christ not like a child. My faith came through the crucible of doubts."

3. Dostoevsky identifies Lizaveta as a *yurodivi*—a Holy Fool or Fool-of-Christ, a kind of saint much loved by many Orthodox Christians. See the chapter on Holy Fools in *Praying With Icons* by Jim Forest (Maryknoll, N.Y.: Orbis Books, 1997).

4. The figure of Fr. Zosima was inspired in part by Fr. Amvrosi, a monk at the Optina Monastery, confessor to countless people. Dostoevsky had gone to see him in 1878 when grieving the death of his two-and-a-half-year-old son, Aleksei. Amvrosi was canonized by the Russian Orthodox Church in 1988. Another model for Zosima was a bishop of the eighteenth century, St. Tikhon of Zadonsk.

5. From the foreword to the Pevear-Volokhonsky translation of *Demons* (New York: Knopf, 1994).

6. From a posting to the Orthodox Peace Fellowship List, an e-mail discussion forum, dated 20 April 2001.

Tools for Examining Conscience

1. Fr. Thomas Hopko, introduction to *A Manual of Communion Prayers,* published by the Monastery of the Holy Myrrhbearers, Otego, N.Y.

2. "Third Century on Love," no. 80, *The Philokalia*, trans. G. E. H. Palmer, Philip Sherrard, and Kallistos Ware (London: Faber & Faber, 1981), II: 96.

3. "First Century on Love," no. 92, *The Philokalia*, II: 63.

4. Fr. John Breck, *The Sacred Gift of Life: Orthodox Christianity and Bioethics* (Scarsdale, N.Y.: St. Vladimir's Seminary Press, 1998), 46-47.

5. Section 16, biblical citations removed.

6. Regarding abortion, see Michael Gorman, *Abortion and the Early Church* (Eugene, Oreg.: Wipf & Stock, 1999). A chapter of the book is posted on the web at <www.incommunion.org/gorman.htm>.

7. The text that follows condenses sections of my book, *The Ladder of the Beatitudes* (Maryknoll, N.Y.: Orbis Books, 1999).

8. John Climacus, "Step 7, 'On Mourning,'" *The Ladder of Divine Ascent*, trans. Colm Luibheid and Norman Russell (New York: Paulist Press, 1982), 145.

9. St. John Chrysostom, "Sermons on Matthew," 54, 7.

10. St. John Chrysostom, "On the Gospel of St. Matthew," 50, iii (PG 58, 508).

11. Fr. Alexander Schmemann, *Great Lent* (Scarsdale, N.Y.: St. Vladimir's Seminary Press, 1974), 34.

12. Olivier Clément, *Three Prayers* (Scarsdale, N.Y.: St. Vladimir's Seminary Press, 2000).

13. Fr. Alexander Schmemann, *Great Lent,* 36.

14. Ibid., 79.

Finding a Confessor

1. For details about St. Amvrosy's life, see *Staretz Amvrosy* by John Dunlop (Scarsdale, N.Y.: St. Vladimir's Seminary Press, 1988).

2. Fr. Alexander Schmemann, *St. Vladimir's Seminary Quarterly.*

3. Bishop Kallistos Ware, "Approaching Christ the Physician."

4. Valentine Zander, *Saint Seraphim of Sarov*, trans. Sr. Gabriel Anne, S.S.C. (Scarsdale, N.Y.: St. Vladimir's Seminary Press, 1975), 55.

5. The scene is described, with many details about Fr. Matthew, in the final chapter of Henri Troyat's biography of Gogol, *Divided Soul.*

6. *Butler's Lives of the Saints*, entry for November 19.

True Confessions

1. *The Journals of Father Alexander Schmemann 1973–1983* (Scarsdale, N.Y.: St. Vladimir's Seminary Press, 2000).
2. Fr. Lorenzo Albacete, professor of theology at St. Joseph's Seminary in Yonkers, writing in the *New York Times Sunday Magazine*, 7 May 2000.
3. Bishop Kallistos Ware, "Approaching Christ the Physician."
4. Ibid.
5. From "The Good Confessor" by Fr. John Udics, Dean of the Diocese of Eastern Pennsylvania, Orthodox Church in America, Secane, PA 19018; e-mail: johnu211@voicenet.com.
6. Fr. Alexander Elchaninov, *The Diary of a Russian Priest* (London: Faber & Faber, 1967), 214, 219.
7. Fr. Lev Gillet, *Serve the Lord with Gladness: Basic Reflections on the Eucharist and the Priesthood* (Scarsdale, N.Y.: St. Vladimir's Seminary Press, 1990), 92-93.
8. From a sermon by Metropolitan Anthony Bloom of London, 5 December 1999.
9. Walker Percy, "Is a Theory of Man Possible?" *Signposts in a Strange Land* (New York: Farrar Straus & Giroux, 1991).